CRACKING
THE BIBLE'S
NUMERIC
CODE

CRACKING THE BIBLE'S NUMERIC CODE

How to Interpret the Numbers of the Bible

Dr. R. J. Gannaway

iUniverse, Inc.
New York Lincoln Shanghai

Cracking the Bible's Numeric Code
How to Interpret the Numbers of the Bible

iUniverse books may be ordered through booksellers or by contacting:

iUniverse
2021 Pine Lake Road, Suite 100
Lincoln, NE 68512
www.iuniverse.com
1-800-Authors (1-800-288-4677)

The views expressed in this work are solely those of the author and do not necessarily reflect the views of the publisher, and the publisher hereby disclaims any responsibility for them.
All scriptures quoted in this book are from *The Living Bible*, used with permission from Tyndale House Publishers of Wheaton, Illinois.
The Ten Plagues table used in the Chapter One—Pertaining to God, was excerpted from the Ryrie Study Bible Expanded Edition, by Charles Caldwell Ryrie, Th.D., Ph.D., used with permission from Moody Publishers of Chicago, Illinois.

ISBN-13: 978-0-595-41150-4 (pbk)
ISBN-13: 978-0-595-85510-0 (ebk)
ISBN-10: 0-595-41150-9 (pbk)
ISBN-10: 0-595-85510-5 (ebk)

Printed in the United States of America

For my wife, Lauren,
who encouraged me to complete this book.
I love you.

Contents

Introduction

Have you ever noticed the recurrence of certain numbers in the Bible? Anyone who has read much of the Bible probably has observed this phenomenon. But have you realized that certain numbers not only recur, but also seem to reappear in similar contexts? Without knowing what to look for, and without keys for understanding, the average Bible reader may assume that numbers in the Bible occur randomly. In fact, numbers in the Bible appear anything but randomly.

This assertion does not imply that every number in the Bible holds symbolism. But as I will explore in later chapters, significant numbers do have associated meanings that add dimension to their use. God, as author of the Bible, uses numbers to interconnect his word. They provide continuity from book to book and from Old Testament to New Testament. Considering that the Old Testament was written in Hebrew and the New Testament was written in Greek, it is quite amazing that the same numbers carry the same meanings over and over. When you remember that there is a large number of authors and their backgrounds are so diverse, the numbers of the Bible become miraculous. In fact, the analysis of these numbers proves conclusively that God is the one and only author of the Bible.

Studying the meanings associated with numbers in the Bible brings you closer to God the author. By learning the symbolism and structure of the divine numeric code, you come closer to God's message and his intent for mankind. It is like walking up to a window and opening it, letting light flood into the room. Everything becomes clearer, as if you were seeing it for the first time.

However noble this study, it can be easily distorted by detractors who would call it *numerology*. Is this study numerology? No, at least it is not numerology in the modern sense of the word. Currently, numerology is associated with the occult, and the meanings given to numbers in modern numerology are unlike those used in the Bible and have different purposes. You know from scripture that Satan distorts godly things. Likewise, numerology is a distortion of what you will discover chapter by chapter in this book. It is a poor reflection meant to divert you from the true path, but it does not take away from the divine use of numbers in the Bible.

Biblical scripture is often given multiple interpretations and therefore frequently remains a mystery. Christianity began as a denomination of Judaism, and Islam arose from both Judaism and Christianity, but now the three religions are distinct and separate even though they have the same roots in the Old Testament. Biblical scholars disagree, and different denominations of Christianity rise up against one another. It is as if a fog constantly changes the image you are attempting to see. How are you to clear away the fog? One way to unravel the mystery rests in how God uses numbers.

I have been a student of the Bible for over forty years. My studies have provided me with the opportunity to teach classes on the relationship of the Old and New Testaments, Old Testament Messianic prophecies, and Bible symbolism. My doctorate in operations research emphasized systems theory and numerical analysis—understanding the patterns in numbers. I can still remember the first time I heard a sermon referencing the use of the number seven in scripture. I suppose it followed easily that I would apply my experience and skills to cracking the numeric code of the Bible.

Understanding the divine meaning of numbers has enhanced my pleasure from reading scripture, and it can do the same for you. For example, if you understood the meaning of biblical numbers, you could decipher the solution to the puzzle posed in the thirteenth chapter of the book of The Revelation:

> Here is a puzzle that calls for careful thought to solve it. Let those who are able, interpret this code: the numeric values of the letters in his name add to 666! (The Revelation 13:18)

The chapters following this one will act as a wind to clear away the fog from the numbers of the Bible by explaining the symbolism of each number and supporting that explanation with examples from the Bible. This description is then amplified by showing how each number logically builds on the preceding number(s) to produce a new meaning.

There are a few simple tools you will need to know how to use and terms you will need to understand before proceeding. For example, what do I mean by the term *number*? When I refer to a number, most often I mean a single digit, ignoring zero—that is: the numbers one, two, three, four, five, six, seven, eight, or nine. Zero is not part of the divine numeric code since it was unknown to the ancient Hebrews and Greeks. While zero or an empty place value (as in 10 or 100) was used by the Babylonians as early as 400 BCE, zero was not used as a numeral until about 650 CE in India. Over the following 600 years, zero as a number spread through the Arabic countries and into Europe, but this was well past the time of biblical scripture. For the purposes of this book, zero represents a null or nothingness. The core numeric code of the Bible, then, consists simply of the numbers *one, two, three, four, five, six, seven, eight*, and *nine*.

But do not most numbers have multiple digits? Of course, but I will rectify that situation by adopting the following simple practice: when the original number contains more than one digit, derivation of a single-digit number is achieved by adding the digits that comprise the original number until only a single digit remains. For example:

$$1 = 1 \qquad\qquad 4 = 4$$

$$10 = 1 + 0 = 1 \qquad\qquad 40 = 4 + 0 = 4$$

$$100 = 1 + 0 + 0 = 1 \qquad\qquad 400 = 4 + 0 + 0 = 4$$

$$123 = 1 + 2 + 3 = 6 \qquad\qquad 456 = 4 + 5 + 6 = 15$$

$$= 1 + 5 = 6$$

In some cases, the number preceding the resolution to a single digit is also significant. The number 456, in the last example above, results in the number 15 before finally producing the number six. This intermediate result did not have to be 15. It could have been 24, 33, 42, or 51. As I will show in the examples that follow, sometimes this intermediate result occurs often enough to be significant on its own to the biblical reader.

Symbolic Numeric Systems

For your analysis of the numeric code of the Bible, you must go beyond the explicit occurrence of numbers and include the numeric values of words and phrases as well. The English language uses Arabic numerals to represent digits, which allows mathematical functions to be performed with great ease. That advantage to mathematics did not come without a cost. Ancient numeric systems used letters to represent numbers. While mathematical functions were more difficult, the ancient systems made it possible for deep symbolism to be embedded in a word or phrase through the inclusion of numeric values that themselves had meanings.

In English, *denotation* is the explicit meaning of a word, and *connotation* refers to the suggested or implied meaning of a word. A word with one denotation may have varied connotations to people who have different backgrounds or who come from different parts of the country. For example, you know the word *dog* to refer to a familiar household pet. But to one person, the word might carry a connotation of loose morals. For another, it might connote unattractiveness. To still another, it could connote a show-off.

The graphic below illustrates the two dimensions of denotation and connotation associated with a word. If you consider the words on this page as two-dimensional, you could think of the denotation as the horizontal dimension—across the page—and you could consider the connotation as the vertical dimension—up and down the page.

Connotation
Implied Meaning

Word

Denotation
Explicit Meaning

As illustrated below, the ancient systems had the potential of an additional dimension of symbolism derived from the numeric code. Embedding the numeric symbolism in the words and phrases allowed ancient writers to add a third dimension, as if the words extended out of the page like a twenty-first century hologram. This additional dimension allowed for a richness of expression lost in today's systems. I will show in later chapters that this symbolism occurs very deliberately throughout the Bible.

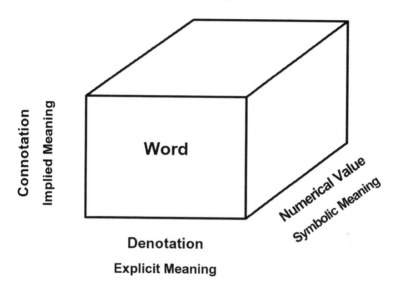

Roman Numbers

How can anyone convert words or phrases into numbers? Since long before Christ, the Hebrews and Greeks used letters of the alphabet to express numbers. This concept is better known with the Roman numeral system:

$$
\begin{array}{rcl}
I & = & 1 \\
V & = & 5 \\
X & = & 10 \\
L & = & 50 \\
C & = & 100 \\
D & = & 500 \\
M & = & 1000
\end{array}
$$

Anyone who has attempted multiplication with complex Roman numerals can attest to the mathematical difficulty associated with using letters to represent numbers. On the other hand, because the Romans used some of their letters to represent numbers, you can use this code to assign a numeric value to Latin words and phrases. I have included two examples below:

Tempus Fugit

Tempus	Fugit
M	I
1000	1

Total = 1001

$$= 1 + 0 + 0 + 1$$

$$= 2$$

Carpe Diem

Carpe		Diem	
C	D	I	M
100	500	1	1000

Total = 100 + 1501 = 1601

$$= 1 + 6 + 0 + 1$$

$$= 8$$

Since the Romans assigned numeric values to so few letters you could point out that it is quite a stretch to assign a numeric value or an associated symbolic meaning to a Latin word or phrase. However, the ancient Hebrew and Greek systems assigned a numeric value to every letter in their alphabets. When each letter in an alphabet possesses a numeric value, the value of the word or phrase can be calculated much more conclusively. The potential for symbolism in a word becomes much greater.

The Languages of the Bible

Why is the numeric symbolism of Latin unimportant, but the symbolism in the Hebrew and Greek numeric systems very important? The answer is simple; the Bible was not written in Latin, but was written in Hebrew and Greek. The entire Old Testament, with the exception of small parts of Ezra, Daniel, and Jeremiah, was written in Hebrew. Those few parts were written in Aramaic. Hebrew was the native language of the writers of the Old Testament when it was written, starting in about 1450 BCE and stretching over a period of one thousand to twelve hundred years. In the last five hundred years before the time of Jesus, Aramaic supplanted Hebrew as a spoken language. In Jesus' time, Hebrew was a dead language—read and sometimes written, but not spoken. Hebrew consisted of 22 letters, all of which were consonants. It was up to the reader to supply the vowel sounds. Since Hebrew was not a spoken language for many centuries, no one today is sure how the words of the Bible were pronounced. Scholars have attempted to recreate the pronunciation, but no one is completely certain of the accuracy.

If Aramaic supplanted Hebrew, then why was the New Testament written in Greek and not Aramaic? In the Roman Empire, the Greek dialect of *Koine*, not Latin, was the common language. Koine Greek was the spoken language of the empire of Alexander the Great. As the Romans conquered the remnants of Alexander's empire, they absorbed Koine Greek as the common language of their empire. Most people who spoke multiple languages knew their native language and Koine Greek. Even the Old Testament had been translated into Koine Greek some 200 years earlier, and it was the most popular version throughout the Greco-Roman world. Koine was the original language of the New Testament. It consisted of 24 letters, including vowels.

Hebrew Numbers

As indicated above, biblical Hebrew, written from right to left, originally contained 22 letters. Each letter in the alphabet was also used to represent a number. Some letters were written differently if they were the last letter in the word. These variant forms were used later to represent larger numbers, but they were not used as numbers when the Bible was written. The table below shows the Hebrew alphabet with the names of the letters and the numbers represented by each letter.

Tet	Het	Zayin	Vav	Heh	Dalet	Gimel	Bet	Aleph
ט	ח	ז	ו	ה	ד	ג	ב	א
9	8	7	6	5	4	3	2	1

Tsade	Pe	Ayin	Samekh	Nun	Mem	Lamed	Kaf	Yod
צ	פ	ע	ס	נ	מ	ל	כ	י
90	80	70	60	50	40	30	20	10

					Tav	Shin	Resh	Qof
					ת	ש	ר	ק
					400	300	200	100

Tsade-F	Pe-F	Nun-F	Mem-F	Kaf-F
ץ	ף	ן	ם	ך
900	800	700	600	500

Biblical Hebrew numbers were formed by selecting the Hebrew letter with the largest numeric value less than the number to be written. Then the largest valued letter less than the remainder of the number to be written would be selected, and so on, until the entire number was formed. The Hebrew numeric system was not a position-based system, just a summation of the values of each letter. It was positional only in the sense the letters were most often written with the highest valued letters from right to left. Of course, there were exceptions. Since letters were being used for numbers, some numbers could be formed with combinations of letters that would spell words that were too sacred or too vulgar to be used. For example, the name of God would never be used to represent a number. In those cases, the order of the letters would be changed. The change of order would not change the value of the number.

Since every Hebrew letter had an associated numeric value, you can calculate a total numeric value for every Hebrew word or name in the Old Testament. Look at the name Moses in Hebrew, which is מ שׁ ה:

מ = 40

שׁ = 300

ה = 5

Total Value = 345

I will show the numerical symbolism of the name Moses when I explore the symbolism of the number *three*.

Greek Numbers

The Old Testament was written in Hebrew, but the New Testament was written in Greek. As in the Hebrew numeric system, the Greek numeric system was formed by using the letters of the Greek alphabet. Also, as in the expanded Hebrew system, 27 letters were needed to fill out the ones, tens, and hundreds. There were only 24 letters in the Greek alphabet. One Greek letter, sigma, was written differently if it was the last letter in the word. If the final letter of the word, it became a stigma. Since two more letters were needed, two arbitrary characters, koppa and sampi, were used. They were letters already obsolete by the time the New Testament was written, and they never appear in a Greek word. Though Greek letters were written in both upper case and lower case forms, both forms carried the same numeric value.

Alpha	Beta	Gamma	Delta	Epsilon	Stigma	Zeta	Eta	Theta
A, α	B, β	Γ, γ	Δ, δ	E, ε	ς	Z, ζ	H, η	Θ, θ
1	2	3	4	5	6	7	8	9

Iota	Kappa	Lambda	Mu	Nu	Xi	Omicron	Pi	Koppa
I, ι	K, κ	Λ, λ	M, μ	N, ν	Ξ, ξ	O, o	Π, π	Ϙ
10	20	30	40	50	60	70	80	90

Rho	Sigma	Tau	Upsilon	Phi	Chi	Psi	Omega	Sampi
P, ρ	Σ, σ	T, τ	Y, υ	Φ, φ	X, χ	Ψ, ψ	Ω, ω	ϡ
100	200	300	400	500	600	700	800	900

As with Hebrew, you can calculate a total numeric value for every Greek word or name in the New Testament. Look at the name Jesus in Greek, which is *Ιησους*:

I = 10

η = 8

σ = 200

o = 70

υ = 400

ς = 200

Total Value = 888

The name Jesus is filled with symbolism that I will present in the later chapter on the number *eight*.

Gematria and Isopsephy

The generic term for converting Hebrew words and sentences to numbers is *gematria*. The term for the equivalent practice in Greek is *isopsephy*, though the term gematria is often applied to any practice of converting words to numbers, including Greek words. As indicated above, there is significant evidence that the writers of the Bible, inspired by God, were very much aware of the symbolism associated with numbers in their explicit form and used this symbolism very deliberately in their writings. Similar evidence exists for gematria and isopsephy. The following example is very well-known.

> Then Hiram cast a round bronze tank, *seven and one half* feet high and *fifteen* feet from brim to brim; *forty-five* feet in circumference. (1 Kings 7:23)

This scripture describes some equipment being cast for the Temple. Do you notice anything strange about the numbers used? The circumference of a circle is determined by multiplying the diameter by the number pi, approximately equivalent to 3.14159. If you multiply 15 feet, the diameter in the above scripture, by 3.14159, you get 47.124 feet, which is not close to the 45 feet circumference in the scripture. This discrepancy would be obvious to anyone familiar with the number pi. Instead, it looks like the author believes the value of pi to be 3.0. Many people have pointed to this scripture as a mistake by the writer, who some think was Jeremiah and others believe was King Solomon or someone else. If it was a mistake, could the mistake be attributed to God, as author of the Bible and the one speaking through the writer? But was it a mistake?

A prominent 18th century Jewish rabbi, the Vilna Gaon, proved otherwise. In Jewish tradition, words appearing in portions of the Old Testament are occasionally read differently than they are written. In its written form, the verse uses the word *kava* (Qof, Vav, Heh) for the circumference, but the word is read as *kav* (Qof, Vav). The numerical value of *kava* is 111 (Qof = 100, Vav = 6, Heh = 5), while the numerical value of *kav* is 106 (Kuf = 100, Vav = 6). When you divide the numerical value of the read word into the written word, you get the following equation: 111/106 = 1.047169. If 1.047169 is multiplied by three, the value that the author ostensibly attributes to pi, the result is 3.14151, which closely approximates the true value of pi.

The example above demonstrates the use of gematria by both the writers of the Old Testament and Bible scholars studying the Hebrew texts. Now look at an example of isopsephy and how early Christians applied it to symbols of their faith. The dove has been a symbol of Jesus since the first days of Christianity. Most people believe that symbolism comes from the following scripture:

> Then one day Jesus came from Nazareth in Galilee, and was baptized by John there in the Jordan River. The moment Jesus came up out of the water, he saw the heavens open and the Holy Spirit in the form of a dove descending on him. (Mark 1:9-10)

Is that scripture the reason why the dove persisted as a symbol of Jesus and Christianity among early Christians? The Greek word for dove is *peristera*. What happens when you apply the Greek numeric values to the letters in the word?

dove (peristera)

περιστερα

80 + 5 + 100 + 10 + 200 + 300 + 5 + 100 + 1 = 801

At first glance, you might find nothing remarkable in the sum of the numerical values of the Greek letters. It is simply the number 801. But gematria and isopsephy do not only study the symbolism embedded in the absolute number of a word. They also compare different words of the same value to discover a symbolic relationship. If you compare the numeric value of the word *dove* in Greek to other words and phrases with the same value, you find something very remarkable. One of the names early Christians used when referring to the All Powerful God was The First and The Last. God used the name for himself when speaking to the prophet Isaiah:

> The Lord, the King of Israel, says—yes, it is Israel's redeemer, the Lord of Hosts, who says it—I am the First and the Last; there is no other God. (Isaiah 44:6)

The equivalent in Greek was The Alpha and Omega, a name incorporating the first and last letter of their alphabet. God called himself by that name again when speaking to John in The Revelation:

> "I am Alpha and Omega, the Beginning and Ending of all things," says God, who is the Lord, the All Powerful One who is, and was, and is coming again! (The Revelation 1:8)

Calculate the value of the name Alpha and Omega:

First and Last (Alpha and Omega)

α   ω

$1 + 800 = 801$

The numerical values for the word dove and the name Alpha and Omega are equivalent. Early Christians equated the two, and the dove persisted as a symbol for Jesus Christ. These are just two of many amazing examples of the relationships of words in the Bible to numbers.

There are multiple methodologies practiced in both gematria and isopsephy. In this book, I will employ the standard reduced, methodology. That is, I will assign the numeric equivalent to each letter in the word or phrase and then add the numeric values to get the total value of the word or phrase. Finally, I will reduce the number to a single digit using the same technique described above for explicit occurrences of numbers. I will not explore other methodologies associated with gematria and isopsephy in depth in this book. The general approaches employed in the alternative methodologies, along with a few examples of each, are included in an appendix.

This approach to assigning a numeric value to a name, word, or phrase has been used for thousands of years. In recent years, computers have allowed a more efficient search of the Bible and conversion of names, words, and phrases to numbers. One reference book used as a source on biblical numbers is *Theomatics* written by Jerry Lucas and Del Washburn and first published by Stein and Day Publishers of New

York, New York in 1977. During years of research, Del Washburn used a computer to subdivide biblical scripture and assigned it a numeric value. He determined this numeric value by examining the original Hebrew and Greek texts of the Bible, giving the appropriate number code to each letter in the word or section of scripture, and then adding the values of the number codes to result in a sum total. Since the original book was written, the subject of theomatics has been covered in additional books, papers, and Web sites. I highly recommend the books and associated Web sites to anyone who would wish to continue their study of the numbers of the Bible.

Good Numbers versus Bad Numbers

Have you ever thought of numbers as good or bad? To some extent, you probably have. Everyone has a number or numbers to which he feels closer than others. Many people have so-called *lucky* numbers that bring them comfort or, even better, good fortune. But the numbers of the Bible are not inherently good or bad. Just as every person has both good and bad in him, the numbers of the Bible can symbolize either good or bad. Each number of the Bible contains symbolism around a theme, and each theme contains a spectrum of good and bad.

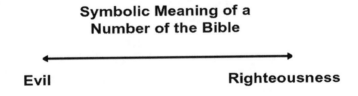

Each number has equal value of righteousness and evil. Numbers tend to be thought of as good or bad because the good symbolism or bad symbolism associated with a number is used more often than its counterpart. A person is a good analogy. It has been argued that a person cannot be all good or all bad. Even the worst person has a little good in him, and the best person is not perfect. Whether the person is considered good or bad depends on the predominant behavior he displays. Similarly, the numbers of the Bible may tend toward good or bad symbolism because of the way they are most commonly used. However, a *bad* number has potential for good and a *good* number has potential for bad. Later on, I will present examples of this phenomenon.

Explicit Numbers versus Implicit Values

In the following chapters, I will refer to both *explicit* numbers and *implicit* values. Explicit numbers are numbers expressed openly in the text but with a symbolic meaning over and above the numeral. This type of example is the easiest for you to see and understand. Not only can you actually see the number, you also have the context of the words and sentences around the number to help in understanding the symbolic meaning.

Implicit value refers to the examination of the original Hebrew and Greek texts of the Bible and assigning the appropriate number code from the ancient systems to each letter in the word or section of scripture. The values of the number codes are added together to result in a sum total and then reduced to a single digit. The implicit value is the numeric equivalent carried within each word or phrase. Since the writers of scripture, inspired by God, were very much aware of this symbolic relationship and exploited it to add meaning to their words, numeric equivalence of words and phrases is not coincidental. Neither is the equivalence in symbolic meaning of those implicit values with their explicit counterparts. In some cases, I will review the original Hebrew and Greek spellings of words and names in the Old and New Testaments. In other cases, I will expand upon this analysis to review patterns identified by Del Washburn in *Theomatics*.

By drawing on the explicit use of numbers and the implicit values of Hebrew and Greek words, names, and sections of scriptures, you will not only be able to examine the numbers quoted in Biblical scripture but will also be able to explore the numeric code embedded in the words of the scripture.

One

Pertaining To God

How would you expect God to structure the numbering system he uses in the Bible? Would it be overly complex, as a reflection of the supreme intellect of God? Or would it follow some pattern discernible only by the most reverent of religious leaders? God's message to his followers has never been hidden. On the contrary, his Son came as a carpenter who preached his message to the masses by using stories they would easily understand. In a similar manner, God's numeric code is simple and logical. It makes sense that the first number pertains to the *one* and only God.

The number *one* is different from all other numbers in that through addition to itself it creates the other numbers, but no matter how many times it is multiplied by itself, it remains the same. As such, the number *one* represents the *one* God omnipresent. It also symbolizes the individual relationship that each person has with the *one* God, the Father of man. And, an individual multiplied over and over results in *one* brotherhood of man.

How do I know the number *one* carries this symbolism? The number *one* appears many times in the Bible, and its meaning is certain. Some examples of its occurrence and significance follow, but the number *one* does not have to appear explicitly to communicate its message. Take, for example, the *10* (1 + 0 = *1*) plagues on the Egyptians. Never is the number *10* used in scriptures to describe the plagues, but all you have to do is count them to see that there were *10*. Why *10* and not some other number such as nine or eleven? God sent these plagues to reveal himself to Pharaoh and the Egyptians so they would let his people go:

> Say to him, "Jehovah, the God of the Hebrews, has sent me back to demand that you let His people go to worship Him

in the wilderness. You wouldn't listen before, and now the Lord says this: 'You are going to find out that I am God ...'" (Exodus 7:16-17)

God sent his **10** plagues to show the superiority of the *one* God of the Hebrews over the many gods of the Egyptians. As you may remember, the Egyptians considered all of the plagues as unusual but natural occurrences until the *tenth* (1 + 0 = **1**) plague.

Plague	Egyptian Gods Involved
1. Nile River to Blood	Hapi—spirit of the Nile Khnum—guardian of the Nile
2. Frogs	Heqt—form of a frog Hapi—spirit of the Nile
3. Swarms of Gnats	Perhaps attack on Egyptian priests
4. Flies	Uatchit—a god who manifested himself as a fly
5. Disease on the Cattle	Apis, Ptah, Mnrvis, Hathor—sacred bulls and cows
6. Boils/Sores on Man and Animal	Serapis and Sekhmet—god and goddess with power to heal.
7. Destruction of Crops and Cattle by Hail	Seth—protector of crops Nut—sky goddess
8. Destruction of Crops by Locusts	Isis—goddess of life Seth—protector of crops
9. Darkness	Re—run god Atum—god of setting sun

| **10**. Death of the | Osiris—giver of life |
| Firstborn | Pharaoh—also considered a deity |

God, through Moses and the **10** plagues, convinced Pharaoh of the existence and power of the *one* God. There are many other examples where the number *one* carries similar symbolism. The following sections quote biblical scripture to build the symbolic meaning of the number *one*. It is important for you to remember that the numbers 10 (1 + 0 = *1*), 100 (1 + 0 + 0 = *1*), and 1000 (1 + 0 + 0 + 0 = *1*) are all equivalent to the number *one*.

One **God**

As in the story of the Egyptian plagues, the number *one* occurs repeatedly in scripture to distinguish the *one* true God from the many pretenders, false gods, and idols of the day. The true God does not have human foibles. He does not have hordes of offspring wreaking havoc on the world. He is not represented in stone or precious metals. He is *one* God everlasting and unchanging.

There is only *one* God:

… there is only *one* God and no other. (Mark 12:32)

O, Israel, listen. Jehovah is our God, Jehovah *alone*. (Deuteronomy 6:4)

… we all know an idol is not really a god, and that there is only *one* God, and no other. (1 Corinthians 8:4)

"When you are calling me good, you are calling me God," Jesus replied, "for God *alone* is truly good." (Matthew 19:17)

And in the future there will continue to be only *one* God:

> And the Lord shall be King over all the earth. In that day there shall be *one* Lord—His name alone will be worshiped. (Zechariah 14:9)

God has only *one* son:

> For God loved the world so much that he gave His *only* Son so that anyone who believes in him shall not perish but have eternal life. (John 3:16)

> But we know there is only *one* God, the Father, who created all things and made us to be His own; and *one* Lord Jesus Christ, who made everything and gives us life. (1 Corinthians 8:6)

God and his Son are *one*:

> I and the Father are *one*. (John 10:30)

And Jesus says the same of his relationship with his disciples:

> I have given them the glory you gave me—the glorious unity of being *one*, as we are—I in them and you in me, all being perfected into *one*. (John 17:22)

Items with Direct Relationships to God

Like a beacon, the number *one* shines through the mist to represent the singularity of God. But are the above examples enough to convince you that the number *one* possesses an embedded symbolism of an association with God? After all, if there is only *one* God, then it is natural that the number *one* would appear in that context. Even more amazing is that anything directly associated with God carries the same symbolism buried in the use of the numeric code. And this symbolism does not occur exclusively in the Old Testament or in the New Testament. The examples below are passages from both the Old and New Testaments intermingled to demonstrate the miraculous use of the number *one*.

His Law was constructed in *10* (1 + 0 = *1*) commandments:

> … God wrote out the Covenant—the *Ten* Commandments—on the stone tablets. (Exodus 34:28)

Exodus 20:1-17
1. I am Jehovah your God who liberated you from your slavery in Egypt. You may worship no other god than me.

2. You may not make yourselves any idols: any images resembling animals, birds, or fish. You must never bow to an image or worship it in any way.

3. You shall not use the name of Jehovah your God irreverently, nor use it to swear to a falsehood.

4. Remember to observe the Sabbath as a holy day. *Six* days a week are for your daily duties and your regular work, but the *seventh* day is a day of Sabbath rest before the Lord your God.

5. Honor your father and mother, that you might have a long, good life in the land the Lord your God will give you.

6. You must not murder.

7. You must not commit adultery.

8. You must not steal.

9. You must not lie.

10. You must not be envious of your neighbor's house, or want to sleep with his wife, or want to own his slaves, oxen, donkeys, or anything else he has.

While everyone is aware of the *Ten* Commandments, few are aware that there are *613* (6 + 1 + 3 = 10, 1 + 0 = *1*) commandments in the Torah. These commandments together are known as the *Mitzvot*, or *Taryag Mitzvot*, with *taryag* representing a pronunciation of the letters that make up the number *613*. Ancient Hebrews lived their lives according to these laws, not just the Ten Commandments. But it is *one* Law:

> For the whole Law can be summed up in this *one* command: "Love others as you love yourself." (Galatians 5:14)

God's house was in *one* piece:

> … so that the Tabernacle, the dwelling place of God, becomes a *single* unit. (Exodus 26:6)

One tenth of the Jews who returned to Judah after their captivity in Babylon were selected to live in Jerusalem, God's holy city:

> The Israeli officials were living in Jerusalem, the Holy City, at this time; but now a *tenth* of the people from the other cities and towns of Judah and Benjamin were selected by lot to live there too. (Nehemiah 11:1)

God's portion of his people's produce is *one tenth*:

> A *tenth* of the produce of the land whether grain or fruit, is the Lord's. (Leviticus 27:30)

God's altar is holy:

> *Once* a year Aaron must sanctify the altar, smearing upon its horns the blood of the sin offering for atonement. This shall be

a regular, annual event from generation to generation, for this is the Lord's supremely holy altar. (Exodus 30:10)

As is God's offering:

> ... and *one* loaf of bread, *one* cake, of shortening bread, and *one* wafer from the basket of unleavened bread that was placed before the Lord: Place these in the hands of Aaron and his sons, to wave them in a gesture of offering to the Lord. (Exodus 29:23-24)

Jesus' robe was sewn from *one* piece of cloth:

> But they said, "Let's not tear up his robe," for it was seamless. (John 19:24)

God's Family, His Church

You have just begun your journey through the numbers of the Bible, yet the probability of the same number applying with the same meaning in so many verses of the Bible is already so remote as to seem impossible. But the same numeric code that applies to the *one* God also miraculously applies to his family—the brotherhood of man, his church.

All of the earth's people descended from *one* man and are of *one* blood:

> He created all of the people of the world from *one* man. (Acts 17:26)

One man brought death to everyone, and *one* man removed death's sting:

> I noticed there was *one* thing that happened to wise and foolish alike—just as the fool will die, so will I. (Ecclesiastes 2:14-15)

The sin of this *one* man, Adam, caused death to be king overall, but all who will take God's gift of forgiveness and acquittal are kings of life because of this *one* man, Jesus Christ. (Romans 5:17)

Nor has He offered himself again and again, as the high priest down here on earth offers animal blood in the Holy of Holies each year. If that had been necessary, then He would have had to die again and again ever since the world began. But no! He came *once* for all, at the end of the age, to put away the power of sin forever by dying for us.

And just as it was destined that man die only *once*, and after that comes judgment, so also Christ died and only *once* as an offering for the sins of many people. (Hebrews 9:25-28)

All believers are of *one* family with the same father:

We are children of the *same* father, Abraham, all created by the *same* God. (Malachi 2:10)

I have other sheep, too, in another fold. I must bring them also, and they will heed my voice; and there will be *one* flock with *one* Shepherd. (John 10:16)

No matter how many of us there are, we all eat from the same loaf, showing that we are all parts of the *one* body of Christ. (1 Corinthians 10:17)

Our bodies have many parts, but the many parts make up only *one* body when they are all put together. So it is with the 'body' of Christ. Each of us is a part of the *one* body of Christ. Some of us are Jews, some are Gentiles, some are slaves and some are free. But the Holy Spirit has fitted us all together into *one* body. (1 Corinthians 12:12-13)

We are parts of *one* body, we have the same spirit, and we have all been called to the same glorious future. For us there is only *one* Lord, *one* faith, *one* baptism, and we all have the same God and Father who is over us all, and living through every part of us. (Ephesians 4:4-6)

We are no longer Jews or Greeks or slave or free men or even merely men or women, but we are all the same—we are Christians; we are *one* in Jesus Christ. (Galatians 3:28)

All the believers were of *one* heart and mind, and no one felt that what he owned was his own; everyone was sharing. (Acts 4:32)

Importance of the Individual

Since everyone is part of the same body, God cannot ignore an individual any more than you could ignore *one* of your arms or *one* of your organs. Therefore, each and every individual is on the same symbolic spectrum with God. As the prodigal son is welcomed home by his earthly father, the Heavenly Father not only welcomes the sinner into his loving arms but constantly reaches out to him so he can hear his word and return to the comfort of the *One*.

Each individual relationship is important:

If a man has a hundred sheep, and *one* wanders away and is lost, what will he do? Won't he leave the ninety-nine others to go out into the hills to search for the lost *one*? (Matthew 18:12)

Little children are especially dear:

But if any of you causes *one* of these little ones who trusts in me to lose his faith, it would be better for you to have a rock tied to your neck and be thrown into the sea.

Beware that you don't look down upon a single *one* of these little children. (Matthew 18:6, 10)

A close relationship with God is the highest goal of the believer:

The *one* thing I want from God, the thing I want most of all, is the privilege of meditating in His temple, living in His presence every day of my life, delighting in His incompatible perfections and glory. (Psalms 27:4)

Implicit Values

In the preceding scriptures, the number *one* is expressed openly in the text but with a symbolic meaning over and above the numeral. What number would you expect to find when you calculate the implicit values of scriptures associated with God, his church, and the importance of the individual? What if the number that resulted was the number *one*? What an amazing truth that would be if there was a relationship between the implicit values of these scriptures and the symbolism associated with the explicit use of the number *one*. Well there is more than a relationship. The explicit and implicit values are the same.

Take the first verse of the Bible:

In the beginning God created the heavens and earth ... (Genesis 1:1)

בראשיח ברא אלהים את תשמים ואת הארץ

The implicit value of this scripture = 2 + 200 + 1 + 300 + 10 + 400 + 2 + 200 + 1 + 1 + 30 + 5 + 10 + 40 + 1 + 400 + 5 + 300 + 40 + 10 + 40 + 6 + 1 + 400 + 5 + 1 + 200 + 90 = 2701.

Now watch: 2 + 7 + 0 + 1 = 10

1 + 0 = *1*

Here are some other examples:

… the image of God. (2 Corinthians 4:4)

εικων Θεου

Implicit Value = 5 + 10 + 20 + 800 + 50 + 9 + 5 + 70 + 400
= 1369

1 + 3 + 6 + 9 = 19

1 + 9 = 10

1 + 0 = *1*

… Son of God … (Galatians 2:20)

υιου του Θεου

Implicit Value = 400 + 70 + 10 + 400 + 300 + 70 + 400 + 9 +
5 + 70 + 400 = 2134

2 + 1 + 3 + 4 = 10

1 + 0 = *1*

… Messiah will come—the one they call the Christ … (John 4:25)

Μεσσιας ερχεται ο λεγομενος Χριστος

Implicit Value = 40 + 5 + 200 + 200 + 10 + 1 + 200 + 5 + 100
+ 600 + 5 + 300 + 1 + 10 + 70 + 30 + 5 + 3 + 70 + 40 + 5 + 50
+ 70 + 200 + 600 + 100 + 10 + 200 + 300 + 70 + 200 = 3700

3 + 7 + 0 + 0 = 10

1 + 0 = *1*

... Kingdom of God ... (Luke 6:20)

Βασιλεια του Θεου

Implicit Value = 2 + 1 +200 + 10 + 30 + 5 + 10 + 1 + 300 + 70 + 400 + 9 + 5 + 70 + 400 = 1513

1 + 5 + 1 + 3 = 10

1 + 0 = *1*

... the Way ... (John 14:6)

η οδος

Implicit Value = 8 + 70 + 4 + 70 + 200 = 352

3 + 5 + 2 = 10

1 + 0 = *1*

The Implicit Value 37

Many who have analyzed the implicit values of words and phrases have discovered a miraculous correlation between phrases associated with Jesus and the implicit values of 111 and 37. The number 111 I will address in a later chapter, but the number 37 belongs here. The number 37 is a prime number divisible only by the number *one* and itself, and the total of its two digits is 10 which is equivalent to *one*. 37 is said to be *the heart* of scripture:

Ha Lev (The Heart)

הלב

Implicit Value = 5 + 30 + 2 = 37

$$3 + 7 = 10$$

$$1 + 0 = \textbf{1}$$

As I indicated in the introduction of this book, there are times when the digits that form the intermediate result are also significant to the message. What are the two digits in question here? As you will learn later, the number *three* has an association with acts of God and the number *seven* with perfection. Given the individual digits and their total, the number 37 refers to an act of God resulting in perfection—Jesus Christ. And Jesus Christ is the Son of God, that is, the embodiment of God.

The implicit values of the examples which follow are all multiples of 37, the most amazing of which is the image of God, which actually is equal to the number 37 squared:

... the image of God. (2 Corinthians 4:4)

εικων Θεου

Implicit Value = 5 + 10 + 20 + 800 + 50 + 9 + 5 + 70 + 400 = 1369

$$1369 = \textbf{37 * 37}$$

... Messiah will come—the one they call the Christ ... (John 4:25)

Μεσσιας ερχεται ο λεγομενος χριστος

Implicit Value = 40 + 5 + 200 + 200 + 10 + 1 + 200 + 5 + 100 + 600 + 5 + 300 + 1 + 10 + 70 + 30 + 5 + 3 + 70 + 40 + 5 + 50 + 70 + 200 + 600 + 100 + 10 + 200 + 300 + 70 + 200 = 3700

$$3700 = \textbf{37 * 100}$$

For in Christ there is all of God in a human body ... (Colossians 2:9)

οτι εν αυτω κατοικει παν το πληρωμα τησ Θεοτητος

Implicit Value = 70 + 300 + 10 + 5 + 50 + 1 + 400 + 300 + 800 + 20 + 1 + 300 + 70 + 10 + 20 + 5 + 10 + 80 + 1 + 50 + 300 + 70 + 80 + 30 + 8 + 100 + 800 + 40 + 1 + 300 + 8 + 200 + 9 + 5 + 70 + 300 + 8 + 300 + 70 + 200 = 5402

5402 = 37 * 146

The Son of Man ... (Luke 22:22)

υιος του ανθρωπου   .

Implicit Value = 400 + 10 + 70 + 200 + 300 + 70 + 400 + 1 + 50 + 9 + 100 + 800 + 80 + 70 + 400 = 2960

2960 = 37 * 80

Christ is the son of David. (Luke 20:41)

τον Χριστον ειναι Δαυιδ υιον

Implicit Value = 300 + 70 + 50 + 600 + 100 + 10 + 200 + 300 + 70 + 50 + 5 + 10 + 50 + 1 + 10 + 4 + 1 + 400 + 10 + 4 + 400 + 10 + 70 + 50 = 2775

2775 = 37 * 75

Summary

In this chapter, I have shown the meaning of the number *one* in biblical scripture and the additional message it provides to the reader who is aware of this meaning. What do you now know about the symbolism of the number *one*?

- It represents the *one* God omnipresent.

- It also occurs in the context of items with a direct relationship to God.

- Two specific associations with God are the relationship of the individual to God and the relationship of God to his Church.

I have also shown how this symbolic message is embedded in the words of scripture. Scriptures with a message similar to the symbolism of the number *one*, have implicit values which reduce to *one*. Within the implicit values, I have also reported a foundation number—the implicit value of 37—that I will build on in later chapters. This number has a special association with Jesus Christ, who is the embodiment of God.

Thus, you have seen the message in the number and the number in the message. The probability of these explicit and implicit numbers holding the same meaning so often is minuscule when assuming a random placement of numbers. You are forced to conclude that this relationship is by God's design.

Two

Pairs of Opposites

With the first number pertaining directly to God, how could you expect the second number to live up to the same high standard? The second number would have to represent something less supreme. In fact, the number *two* emphasizes this point by referring to pairs of opposites.

You can see the natural connotation reinforced every day—male and female, day and night, black and white, and good and evil. God uses the number *two* in his word in the same simple but powerful manner. Within the spectrum of the meaning of the number *two*, the symbolism can associate with the division of opposites or the union of opposites.

You do not have to read far into the Bible before you run into these concepts. The account of creation in the first chapter of the book of Genesis is marked with division. The first use of the number *two* previews how the number *two* will be used throughout the remainder of the Bible to symbolize opposites, rivals, and good and evil.

> Then God said, "Let there be night." And light appeared. And God was pleased it with it, and *divided* the light from the darkness. So he let it shine for awhile, and then there was darkness again. He called the light "daytime" and the darkness "nighttime." Together they formed the first day.
>
> And God said, "Let the vapors *separate* to form the sky above and the oceans below. So God made the sky, *dividing* the vapor above from the water below. This all happened on the *second* day …
>
> For God made *two* huge lights, the sun and the moon, to shine down upon the earth—the larger one, the sun to preside over the day and the smaller one, the moon, to preside over the night. (Genesis 1:3-8, 16-18)

You are probably aware of the story of creation and Adam and Eve. The number *two* plays a key role in the symbolism of that account. In the first chapter of Genesis, you read about the creation of life on earth distinct and separate from life in heaven. By the second chapter, you read of *two* genders—man and woman—placed in the Garden of Eden with mention of *two* particular trees. The fact that there were *two* trees implies they had opposite results—the Tree of Conscience which brought death and the Tree of Life which promised eternal life:

> Then the Lord planted a garden in Eden, to the east, and placed in the garden the man He had formed. The Lord God planted all sorts of beautiful trees there in the garden, trees producing the choicest of fruit. At the center of the garden He placed the Tree of Life, and also the Tree of Conscience, giving knowledge of Good and Bad. (Genesis 2:8-9)

> Then the Lord God caused the man to fall into a deep sleep, and took *one* of his ribs and closed up the place from which He had removed it, and made the rib into a woman, and brought her to man. (Genesis 2:21-22)

In the third chapter, you read of the first sin, the introduction of evil and death, and the expulsion of man from the Garden. And in the fourth chapter, you read of Abel and Cain symbolizing right and wrong:

> So the Lord God banished him forever from the Garden of Eden, and sent him out to farm the ground from which he had been taken. (Genesis 3:23)

> Then Adam had sexual intercourse with Eve his wife, and she conceived and gave birth to a son, Cain (meaning "I have created"). For, as she said, "With God's help, I have created a man!" Her next child was his brother Abel.
>
> Abel became a shepherd, while Cain was a farmer. At harvest time Cain brought the Lord a gift of his farm produce, and Abel brought the fatty cuts of meat from his best lambs, and presented them to the Lord. And the Lord accepted Abel's

offering, but not Cain's. This made Cain both dejected and very angry, and his face grew dark with fury.

"Why are you angry?" the Lord asked him. "Why is your face so dark with rage? It can be bright with joy if you will do what you should! But if you refuse to obey, watch out. Sin is waiting to attack you, longing to destroy you. But you can conquer it!"

One day Cain suggested to his brother, "Let's go out into the fields." And while they were together there, Cain attacked and killed his brother. (Genesis 4:1-8)

So in the first four chapters of the Bible, you already have the major themes of the number *two*—flesh and spirit, male and female, good and evil, right and wrong. Much of the remainder of the Bible is devoted to the resolution of these opposites.

God and the World

The message of opposites is driven home in the book of Genesis with the story of Abraham and Lot. Abraham kept his faith in God and became the patriarch of the chosen people. Lot, who came from the same family as Abraham, sought worldly gain in the city of Sodom and lost everything. In this way, the Bible contrasts the spiritual believer with the worldly believer.

The message of the scripture is very clear that flesh and spirit are opposites of each other. The term that describes the worldly existence that is opposite to the holy, spiritual existence of God is *carnal*. The carnal world gives in to the appetites of the flesh. While not all worldly desires are bad, they are all carnal. Carnal desires have negative impact when they occur in excess. Examples include hunger and lust. Because of the harm caused by excessively giving in to carnal appetites, the term carnal often carries a negative connotation. Regardless, the carnal body cannot enter the presence of God.

But what about the body of Christ? Though Jesus took physical form while on earth, he could not retain that physical form in the presence of his father. If you remember, immediately following his resurrection, Jesus warns Mary Magdalene:

> "Mary!" Jesus said. She turned toward Him.
> "Master!" she exclaimed.
> Don't touch me!" He cautioned, "For I haven't yet ascended to the Father. But go find My brothers and tell them that I ascend to My Father and your Father, My God and your God." (John 20:16-17)

And earlier in the book of John, Jesus had explained to his disciples that he must die and ascend to his father in order that the disciples would receive the comforter. That is, the physical form must leave in order to allow the spiritual form to come:

> "… I will ask the Father and He will give you another Comforter, and He will never leave you. He is the Holy Spirit, the Spirit who leads into all truth. The world at large cannot receive Him, for it isn't looking for Him and doesn't recognize Him. But you do, for He lives with you now, and some day shall be in you." (John 14:15-17)

Now look at scriptures which contain examples of the number *two* used in this same context. As I indicated earlier, the Bible considers the divine God and the carnal world with all of its pleasures to be opposites:

> You cannot serve *two* masters; God and money. For you will hate one and love the other, or else the other way around. (Matthew 6:24)

Look at the number of soldiers in the army that opposes God at the end of time. Until recently, this number would have been difficult to believe:

> They led an army of *200,000,000* Warriors—I heard an announcement of how many there were. (The Revelation 9:16)
> $(2 + 0 + 0 + 0 + 0 + 0 + 0 + 0 + 0 = 2)$

Male and Female

Have you ever wondered what life would be like with just one gender? How much simpler would life be, yet, at the same time, how monotonous and unfulfilling? In his infinite wisdom, God realized that man was not complete without a mate. Therefore, he caused Adam to fall asleep and from his rib created woman. Since that time, male and female have journeyed through life together.

Man and woman are *two* separate people before marriage, but they become *one* person in the eyes of God following marriage:

> Then the Lord God caused man to fall into a deep sleep, and took *one* of his ribs and closed up the place from which he had removed it, and made the rib into a woman, and brought her to man.
>
> "This is it!" Adam exclaimed. "She is part of my own bone and flesh! Her name is 'woman' because she was taken out of a man." This explains why a man leaves his father and mother and is joined to his wife in such a way that the *two* become *one* person. (Genesis 2:21-24)
>
> ... a man should leave his father and mother, and be forever united to his wife. The *two* become as *one*—no longer *two* but *one*! (Matthew 19:5-6)

Noah brought the majority of the animals onto the ark in *pairs*, male and female:

> Bring the animals, too—a *pair* of each ...
> ... They came into the boat in *pairs*, male and female, just as God commanded Noah. (Genesis 7:2, 9)

The Righteous and Unrighteous

The Bible has many references to the *righteous* and the *unrighteous*. Those people who live as God would have them live are the righteous. That is, they live completely by faith—from beginning to end. Because they accept God's gift of salvation through his Son, the righteous maintain good relations between themselves and God. Their faith in the Lord Jesus assures them salvation. Righteousness allows them to live now and forever in the presence of God.

On the other hand, the unrighteous, those people who do not live by faith as god would have them to live, are doomed to the death associated with sin, and they will be separated from the Father forever. They will never live within his presence. Without the bridge of faith in Jesus Christ, there is no way for the unrighteous to traverse the gulf that separates them from the righteous.

The Pharisee and the tax collector illustrate the prayer of the righteous and the prayer of the unrighteous:

> *Two* men went to the Temple to pray. One was a proud, self-righteous Pharisee, and the other a cheating tax collector. The proud Pharisee "prayed" this prayer: "Thank God, I am not a sinner like everyone else, especially like that tax collector over there! For I never cheat, I don't commit adultery, I go without food twice a week, and I give to God a *tenth* of everything I earn."
>
> But the corrupt tax collector stood at a distance and dared not even lift his eyes to heaven as he prayed, but beat upon his chest in sorrow, exclaiming, "God, be merciful to me, a sinner." I tell you, this sinner, not the Pharisee, returned home forgiven! (Luke 18:10-14)

Ten bridesmaids waiting for a bridegroom were divided into *two* groups, the righteous who were prepared for his coming, and the unrighteous who were not prepared:

> "The Kingdom of God can be illustrated by the story of *ten* virgins who took their lamps and went to meet the bridegroom. But only *five* of them were wise enough to fill their lamps with oil, while the other *five* were foolish and forgot ..." (Matthew 25:1-13)

It is better to have *one* righteous hand than one righteous and one unrighteous:

> "If your hand does wrong, cut it off. Better live forever with *one* hand than be thrown into the unquenchable fires of hell with *two*!" (Mark 9:43-44)

Of the *two* thieves crucified with Jesus, one repented and one did not, demonstrating that all may have hope but no one may assume salvation:

> *Two* others, criminals, were led out to be executed with him at a place called "the Skull." There all *three* were crucified—Jesus on the center cross, and the *two* criminals on either side ... One of the criminals hanging beside Him scoffed, "So you're the Messiah, are you? Prove it by saving yourself—and us too, while you're at it!"
>
> But the other criminal protested. "Don't you even fear God when you are dying? We deserve to die for our evil deeds, but this man hasn't done one thing wrong." Then he said, "Jesus, remember me when you come into your kingdom."
>
> And Jesus replied, "Today you will be with me in Paradise." (Luke 23:32-33, 39-43)

At the end of time, the righteous will be separated from the unrighteous:

> *Two* men will be working together in the field, and *one* will be taken, the other left. *Two* women will be going about their household tasks; *one* will be taken, the other left. (Matthew 24:40-41)

Rivals

There was rivalry in the Bible that is still having a dramatic impact on the world today. You may know the story of Abraham and his *two* sons,

Ishmael and Isaac. God made a covenant with Abraham that because Abraham had believed and obeyed God's word, God would make him the father of a great nation. But Abraham grew older without any sons because his wife was barren, and his faith began to weaken. So his wife, Sarah, gave Abraham her Egyptian servant girl, Haggar, to provide him with a son:

> But Sarai and Abram had no children. So Sarai took her maid, an Egyptian girl named Haggar, and gave her to Abram to be his *second* wife ... So Haggar gave Abram a son, and Abram named him Ishmael. (Genesis 16:1-2, 15)

But later in life, Sarah miraculously became pregnant and gave birth to a son. This established a rivalry that exists to this day:

> Then God did as he promised, and Sarah became pregnant and gave Abraham a baby son in his old age, at the time God had said; and Abraham named him Isaac (meaning "Laughter!"). (Genesis 21:1-3)

> Time went on and the child grew and was weaned; and Abraham gave a party to celebrate the happy occasion. But when Sarah noticed Ishmael—the son of Abraham and the Egyptian girl Hagar—teasing Isaac, she turned upon Abraham and demanded, "Get rid of that slave girl and her son. He is not going to share in your property with my son. I won't have it." (Genesis 21:8-10)

Whether they are nations or kingdoms or even brothers, rivals are often paired against one another in the scripture. Of course, the number *two* appears in this context.

Though twins, Jacob and Esau were very different:

> ... it seemed as though children were fighting each other inside her!

"I can't endure this," she exclaimed. So she asked the Lord about it.

And He told her, "The sons in your womb shall become *two* rival nations. *One* will be stronger than the other; and the older shall be a servant of the younger!" (Genesis 25:22-23)

Because he was his father's favorite, Joseph was also considered a rival by his brothers:

So when the traders came by, his brothers pulled Joseph out of the well and sold him to them for *twenty* pieces of silver ... (Genesis 37:28)

Based on what he heard from the magi, King Herod saw the newborn Jesus as a potential rival:

Herod was furious what he learned the astrologers had disobeyed him. Sending soldiers to Bethlehem, he ordered them to kill every boy *two* years old and under ... (Matthew 2:16)

In an effort to avoid executing Jesus, Pilate offered the crowd a choice between Jesus and a criminal:

So when the governor asked again, "Which of these *two* shall I release to you?" the crowd shouted back their reply: "Barabbas!" (Matthew 27:21)

Two Testaments

The Old Testament Law condemned man to death, but the New Testament grace offers life eternal:

The *Ten* Commandments were given so that all could see the extent of their failure to obey God's laws. But the more we see our sinfulness, the more we see God's abounding grace forgiving us. Before, sin ruled over all men and brought them to death, but now God's kindness rules instead, giving us right standing with God and resulting in eternal life through Jesus Christ our Lord. (Romans 5:20-21)

Implicit Values

As you saw with the number *one*, comparing implicit values of scriptures with contexts similar to the symbolic meaning of a number can reinforce your understanding of the message embedded in the numeric code. So what would you expect the implicit value to be when the context refers to opposites or division? How about the number *two*?

The first example I will show comes from the book of Daniel. It is the well-known story of the writing on the wall:

And so God sent those fingers to write this message: 'Mene,' 'Mene,' 'Tekel,' Parsin.'

This is what it means:

"Mene means 'numbered'—God has numbered the days of your reign, and they are ended.

"Tekel means 'weighed'—you have been weighed in God's balances and have failed the test.

"Parsin means *'divided'*—your kingdom will be *divided* and given to the Medes and the Persians." (Daniel 5:24-28)

Mene, tekel, and parsin are Aramaic words associated with coins which in Hebrew were the mina, shekel, and parsim, the plural form of peres (half mina). If you calculate the implicit values for these words, you find the following:

מנה מנה שקל פרסים

Implicit Value = 50 + 40 + 5 + 50 + 40 + 5 + 300 + 100 + 30 + 80 + 200 + 60 + 10 + 40 = 1010

$$1 + 0 + 1 + 0 = 2$$

Along the spectrum of the symbolism associated with the number *two*, you find God's grace—which you can define as favor shown to the unworthy—and you find blasphemy—which you can define as an action against God:

... grace ... (2 Corinthians 4:15)

χαρις

Implicit Value = 600 + 1 + 100 + 10 + 200 = 911

9 + 1 + 1 = 11

1 + 1 = **2**

Blasphemy ... (The Revelation 13:6)

Βλασφημιας

Implicit Value = 2 + 30 + 1 + 200 + 500 + 8 + 40 + 10 + 1 + 200 = 992

9 + 9 + 2 = 20

2 + 0 = **2**

Summary

Thus far, you have explored only the first two numbers of the divine numeric code. You can already see what will be even more evident in the remaining numbers—that the next number in sequence builds on the preceding number. The number *one* symbolizes the perfect God and leads into the number *two* which represents opposites. This theme of opposites is set in the first few chapters of the Bible and runs throughout the remainder of scripture. It is also reinforced in everyday life.

Look once again at the pairs of opposites found in scripture:

- God and the World

- Good and Evil

- Male and Female

- Righteous and Unrighteous

- Right and Wrong

- Old Testament Law and New Testament Grace

- Rivals

These opposites are very powerful messages, and they surround the number *two* in the numeric code of the Bible. With each quote from scripture and each implicit value shown, the proof builds that the Bible had a single divine author who wrote through diverse men's hands.

Three

The Holy Trinity

The number *three* is the second most sacred number in the numeric code (behind only the number *seven*). Like the number *one*, it is associated with God, but while the number *one* pertains to God, the number *three* completes the Holy Trinity. It represents the sum of the number *one* (the Father) plus the number *two* (the Son and Holy Spirit, opposites in flesh and spirit). In addition to relating to the Holy Trinity, the number *three* is associated with actions of God, since such actions were/are manifestations of the Father working through the Son or the Holy Spirit.

The number *three* has a special association with Jesus. This association is appropriate to the Bible's numeric code and is, in fact, one of the greatest examples of the awesome miracle the numeric code represents. After all, the sending of his only Son to earth to die for man was God's greatest act. And the many miracles performed by Jesus during his stay here are the most concentrated series of divine interventions recorded.

Jesus began his ministry at age 30 (3 + 0 = 3) and taught for *three* years. He faced *three* temptations in the desert and was in the tomb *three* days prior to his resurrection. As further explained below, the number *three* appears so often in relation to Jesus' life that the association cannot be random.

Acts of God

Many of the most amazing miracles in both the Old and New Testaments have the number *three* associated with their stories. People such as Gideon, Jonah, Paul, Abraham, and Jesus work God's wonders in stories you may have heard since your childhood. But have you noticed how the number *three* interconnects them like a thread running through a tapestry? Now you can appreciate the numeric code that ties them all together.

God gave Joseph the ability to interpret dreams in order to free him from prison:

> The wine taster told his dream first. "In my dream," he said, "I saw a vine with *three* branches that began to bud and blossom …
>
> "I know what the dream means," Joseph said. "The *three* branches mean *three* days! Within *three* days Pharaoh is going to take you out of prison and give you back your job as his wine taster. And please have some pity on me when you are back in his favor, and mention me to Pharaoh, and ask him to let me out of here …" (Genesis 40:10-14)

The baby Moses was hidden to save him from being killed:

> When the baby's mother saw that he was an unusually beautiful baby, she hid him at home for *three* months. (Exodus 2:2)

Only 300 (3 + 0 + 0 = 3) of the 10,000 (1 + 0 + 0 + 0 + 0 = *1*) men in Gideon's army kept their wits about them in thirst. They lifted water to their mouths such that they could see what was around them, rather than drinking while lying on their stomachs. God selected those 300 (3 + 0 + 0 = 3) men for Gideon's victory over the Midianites:

> Only *three hundred* of the men drank from their hands; all the others drank with their mouths to the stream. I'll conquer the Midianites with these *three hundred!*" the Lord told Gideon. "Send the others home!" (Judges 7:6-7)

When the Spirit came over him, Samson could work wonders:

> So he went out and caught *three hundred* foxes and tied their tails together in pairs, with a torch between each pair. Then he

lit the torches and let the foxes run through the fields of the Philistines, burning the grain to the ground … (Judges 15:4)

God kept Jonah in the whale *three* days during which time Jonah found God's will. Jesus referenced this miracle later to prophecy his own future:

Now the Lord had arranged for a great fish to swallow Jonah. And Jonah was inside the fish *three* days and *three* nights. (Jonah 1:17)

One day some of the Jewish leaders, including some Pharisees, came to Jesus asking Him to show them a miracle.

But Jesus replied, "Only an evil, faithless nation would ask for further proof; and none will be given except what happened to Jonah the prophet! For as Jonah was in the great fish for *three* days and *three* nights, so I, the Son of Man, shall be in the heart of the earth *three* days and *three* nights. (Matthew 12:38-40)

During Paul's conversion, he was blind for *three* days:

As Paul picked himself up off the ground, he found that he was blind. He had to be led into Damascus and was there *three* days, blind, going without food and water all that time. (Acts 9:8-9)

God appeared to Abraham in the form of *three* men on their way to Sodom and Gomorrah:

The Lord appeared to Abraham while he was living in the oak grove at Mamre. This is the way it happened: One hot summer afternoon as he was sitting in the opening of his tent, he suddenly noticed *three* men coming toward him. (Genesis 18:1-2)

At the end of time, the army opposing God will destroy a *third* of mankind with *three* plagues:

> They had been kept in readiness for that year and month and day and hour, and now they were turned loose to kill a *third* of all mankind.
>
> I saw their horses spread out before me in a vision; their riders wore fiery-red breastplates, though some were sky-blue and others yellow. The horses' heads looked much like lions', and *smoke* and *fire* and *flaming sulphur* billowed from their mouths, killing *one-third* of all mankind. (The Revelation 9:15, 17-18)

There were *three* religious feasts that required Jews to make a pilgrimage to the Temple: the feasts of Passover, Weeks (or Pentecost), and Tabernacles:

> There are *three* religious pilgrimages you must make ... At these *three* times each year, every man in Israel shall appear before the Lord God. (Exodus 23:14, 17)

Though prayer was decreed illegal, Daniel continued to pray. After being caught and thrown into the lions' den, Daniel miraculously survived, to the delight of King Darius:

> So King Darius signed the law.
>
> But though Daniel knew about it, he went home and knelt down as usual in his upstairs bedroom, with its windows open toward Jerusalem, and prayed *three* times a day, just as he always had, giving thanks to his God. (Daniel 6:9-10)

Three voices witnessed that Jesus was the Son of God:

> So we have these *three* witnesses: the voice of the Holy Spirit in our hearts, the voice from heaven at Christ's baptism, and the voice before He died. And they all say the same thing: that Jesus Christ is the Son of God. (1 John 5:7-8)

God is love:

> There are *three* things that remain—faith, hope, and love—and the greatest of these is love. (1 Corinthians 13:13)

I have described previously the spectrum of symbolism associated with the numbers of the Bible. Acts of Satan, who is said to have turned *one third* of the angelic host against God, can also be symbolized by the number *three*:

> Suddenly a red Dragon appeared, with *seven* heads and *ten* horns, and *seven* crowns on his heads. His tail drew along behind him a *third* of the stars, which he plunged to the earth. (The Revelation 12:3-4)

Age to Begin God's Service

Think of all the possible ages a person could start his/her service to the Lord. Think of the various ages you began your different jobs or changes of professions. Then think of the ages when your friends and family members made similar decisions. What are the odds that the ages would be the same? It is no simple coincidence that three of God's most notable servants began their service to the Lord at the age of 30 (3 + 0 = 3). It is part of the miracle of the numeric code of the Bible.

Joseph interprets Pharaoh's dream and enters the service of the Lord by serving Pharaoh:

> … So Joseph became famous throughout the land. He was *thirty* years old as he entered the service of the king. (Genesis 41:45-46)

David became king of Judah at *thirty*:

> He had already been the king of Judah for seven years, since the age of *thirty*. (2 Samuel 5:4)

Jesus entered public ministry at the same age:

> Jesus was about *thirty* years old when he began his public ministry. (Luke 3:23)

And though it was not *thirty*, Abraham entered his covenant with God at an age that resolves to the same number *three*:

> After the death of Abram's father, God told him, "Leave your own country behind you, and your own people, and go to the land I will guide you to. If you do, I will cause you to become the father of a great nation; I will bless you and make your name famous, and you will be a blessing to many others. I will bless you and curse those who curse you; and the entire world will be blessed because of you.
>
> So Abram departed as the Lord had instructed Him, and Lot went too; Abram was *seventy-five* years old at that time. (Genesis 12:1-4)

$7 + 5 = 12$

$1 + 2 = 3$

Association with Jesus

As described earlier, the number *three* has a special association with Jesus. This association begins at his birth and continues his whole life. If you know the Christmas story, you have seen images of *three* magi visiting Jesus following his birth in Bethlehem. In fact, no one knows how many magi there were. Different traditions record different numbers from *three* to *twelve*. What most scholars believe is that the magi were aristocratic astrologers. They probably interpreted Jesus' birth from a conjunction of planets. A conjunction is when two or more planets came close enough together in the sky that their brightness increased significantly. Such a conjunction occurred about the time of Jesus' birth.

Though you cannot not know for certain how many magi there were, the Bible records how many gifts they brought—*three*:

> Entering the house where the baby and Mary His mother were, they threw themselves down before Him, worshipping. Then they opened their presents and gave Him *gold, frankincense,* and *myrrh*. (Matthew 2:11)

Traditionally, the gold symbolizes deity; the frankincense represents purity; and the myrrh foretells of death since it was used in embalming. But from a more practical sense, the gold may have financed Jesus' family's flight into Egypt. The frankincense and myrrh may have been brought to Jesus' tomb to prepare his body.

The above example of the association of the number *three* with Jesus is not an explicit occurrence of the number. But there are very many examples of the explicit use of the number *three*. In fact, the association occurs so often that it cannot be random coincidence. Only a few examples follow.

Peter had both expressions of love and denial:

> Once more He asked him, "Simon, son of John, are you my friend?"
>
> Peter was grieved at the way Jesus asked the question this *third* time. "Lord, you know my heart; you know I am," he said. (John 21:17)

> Peter declared, "If everyone else deserts you, I won't."
>
> Jesus told him, "The truth is that this very night, before the clock crows at dawn, you will deny me *three* times!" (Matthew 26:33-34)

Judas Iscariot betrayed Jesus for silver:

> Then Judas Iscariot, one of the *twelve* apostles, went to the chief priests, and asked, "How much will you pay me to get

Jesus into your hand?" And they gave him *thirty* silver coins. (Matthew 26:14-15)

There were *three* crosses at Jesus' crucifixion:

There all *three* were crucified—Jesus on the center cross, and the *two* criminals on either side. (Luke 23:33)

Jesus rose from the grave after *three* days:

Then he began to tell them all about the terrible things he would suffer, and that he would be rejected by the elders and the Chief Priests and the other Jewish leaders—and be killed, and that he would rise again *three* days afterward. (Mark 8:31)

Path to Salvation

When Peter describes the path to salvation at Pentecost, it is described in *three* actions.

And Peter replied, "Each one of you must *turn from sin*, *return to God*, and *be baptized* in the name of Jesus Christ for the forgiveness of your sins; then you shall receive this gift, the Holy Spirit. (Acts 2:38)

The Number 12

The number 12 is a significant, commonly-used number in the Bible. But why would I include it here in a discussion of the number *three* rather than as a separate chapter? Look at the digits, and apply what you have learned. You must add the digits to discover their meaning. The sum of the digits in the number 12 equals *three* (1 + 2 = 3). Therefore, the number 12 is a special use of the number *three*.

As you saw in the example scriptures above, the number *three* symbolizes acts of God. Think of how you remember the number 12 being used in the Bible—the 12 tribes, the 12 disciples, etc. Now that you know that the number 12 is really a form of the number *three*, what can it mean? The number 12 represents the specific act of God choosing his following from among the masses.

Before I get into the explicit uses of the number 12, look at another example that emphasizes the symbolism of being chosen from the masses. This example comes from the book of Judges. The book of Judges recounts the time between Joshua's conquest of most of Palestine and the beginning of the monarchy. During this time, Israel was a loose confederation of independent tribes. The book of Judges describes how the tribes who should have completed their conquest of Palestine instead failed to fully obey God. Rather than driving out the remaining Canaanites, they compromised and suffered as a result.

But why is the book of Judges called by that name? It is because of the leaders that God chose during this period to save his people from their oppressors. As indicated in the *Ryrie Study Bible*, this selection followed a cycle:

Cycle of Judges

1. Israel serves the Lord

2. Israel falls into sin and idolatry

3. Israel is enslaved

4. Israel cries out to the Lord

5. God raises up a judge

6. Israel is delivered

7. Israel serves the Lord again and the cycle repeats

God would raise a judge for a period of time, and then there would be a period of time without a judge before there would again be a need for God to raise a judge. How many judges would you expect God to choose? He chose *twelve* judges. Given that I am referring to a period of time covering well over 300 years and a loose confederation of tribes from which to choose the judges, what is the probability that there would be 12 judges? There were 12 because of the message in God's numbers. Here is the list of judges:

Judges in the Old Testament

1. Othniel	7. Jair
2. Ehud	8. Jephthah
3. Shamgar	9. Ibzan
4. Deborah and Barak	10. Elon
5. Gideon	11. Abdon
6. Tola	*12.* Samson

Now that you have seen how the number 12 was used in the book of Judges, look at some explicit examples in other scriptures.

There are 12 tribes of Israel and 12 disciples:

Twelve Tribes of Israel	**Twelve Disciples of Jesus**
Reuben	Simon Peter
Simeon	James the Greater
Judah	John
Dan	Andrew
Naphtali	Judas Thomas
Gad	Nathanael Bartholomew
Issachar	Philip
Asher	Judas Thaddaeus

Zebulun	Matthew
Benjamin	James the Less
Ephraim	Simon the Zealot
Manasseh	Judas Iscariot

Moses wrote down the laws; and early the next morning he built an altar at the foot of the mountain, with *twelve* pillars around the altar because there are *twelve* tribes of Israel. (Exodus 24:4)

Every Sabbath day the High Priest shall place *twelve* loaves of bread in *two* rows upon the golden table that stands before the Lord. These loaves shall be baked from finely ground flour, using a *fifth* of a bushel for each. Pure frankincense shall be sprinkled along each row. This will be a memorial offering made by fire to the Lord, in memory of His everlasting covenant with the people of Israel. (Exodus 24:5-6)

Jesus called His *twelve* disciples to Him, and gave them the authority to cast out evil spirits and to heal every kind of sickness and disease. (Matthew 10:1)

Look at the calling of Elisha:

So Elijah went and found Elisha who was plowing a field with *twelve* yoke of oxen before him, and he with the *twelfth* ... (1 Kings 19:19)

Jesus was 12 years old when he revealed how special he was:

When Jesus was *twelve* years old He accompanied His parents to Jerusalem for the annual Passover Festival, which they attended each year ...
    ... *Three* days later they finally discovered Him. He was in the Temple, sitting among the teachers of the Law, discussing deep questions with them and amazing everyone with His understanding and answers. (Luke 2:41-42, 46-47)

How many early Christians would you expect to attend a prayer meeting?

> This prayer meeting went on for several days. During this time, on a day when about *120* people were present, Peter stood up and addressed them … (Acts 1:15)

In the future, the Old and New Testaments will come together:

> … you my disciples shall certainly sit on *twelve* thrones judging the *twelve* tribes of Israel. (Matthew 19:28)

And they will reside in a new Jerusalem. It will have 12 gates, each constructed from a single pearl for a total of 12 pearls with the names of the 12 tribes on them. Each gate will have an angel standing guard, for a total of 12 angels. The walls will have 12 foundations garnished with 12 precious stones. The names of the 12 apostles can be found in the foundations. The city is 12,000 furlongs long by 12,000 furlongs wide by 12,000 furlongs high:

> In a vision he took me to a towering mountain peak and from there I watched the wondrous city, the holy Jerusalem, descending out of the skies from God. It was filled with the glory of God, and flashed and glowed like a precious gem, crystal clear and jasper. Its walls were broad and high, with *twelve* gates guarded by *twelve* angels. And the names of the *twelve* tribes of Israel were written on the gates. There were *three* gates on each side—north, south, east, and west.
>
> The walls had *twelve* foundation stones, and on them were written the names of the *twelve* apostles of the Lamb.
>
> The angel held in his hand a golden measuring stick to measure the city and its gates and walls. When he measured it, he found it was a square as wide as it was long; in fact it was in the form of a cube, for its height was exactly the same as its other dimensions—*twelve thousand* furlongs in each way. Then he measured the thickness of the walls and found them to be *one hundred forty four* cubits across.

The city itself was pure, transparent gold like glass! The wall was made of jasper, and was built on *twelve* layers of foundation stones inlaid with gems:

> The first layer was jasper;
> The second with sapphire;
> The third with chalcedony;
> The fourth with emerald;
> The fifth with sardonyx;
> The sixth layer with sardus;
> The seventh with chrysolite;
> The eighth with beryl;
> The ninth with topaz;
> The tenth with chrysoprase;
> The eleventh with jacinth;
> The *twelfth* with amethyst.

The *twelve* gates were made of pearls—each gate from a single pearl! And the main street was pure, transparent gold, like glass.

No temple could be seen in the city, for the Lord God Almighty and the Lamb of God are worshipped in it everywhere. (The Revelation 21:10-22)

Implicit Values

The implicit values resulting in the number *three* are the most numerous of the Bible. If all of their scriptures were collected in one place, they would make a large book by themselves. Here, I will only include some of the more significant examples.

Acts of God captured in scripture often have an implicit value that totals to *three*. God is also so associated with love that he is said to be love:

> … love (1 John 4:8)

αγαπη

Implicit Value = 93

$9 + 3 = 12$

$1 + 2 = 3$

... the Sabbath day. (Luke 13:14)

τη ημερα του σαββατου

Implicit Value = 300 + 8 + 8 + 40 + 5 + 100 + 1 + 300 + 70 + 400 + 200 + 1 + 2 + 2 + 1 + 300 + 70 + 400 = 2208

$2 + 2 + 0 + 8 = 12$

$1 + 2 = 3$

... witness ... (John 1:7)

μαρτυριαν

Implicit Value = 40 + 1 + 100 + 300 + 400 + 100 + 10 + 1 + 50 = 1002

$1 + 0 + 0 + 2 = 3$

The Exodus and the Law came from God through Moses, who God chose to lead his people out of Egypt to the Promised Land:

... Moses ... (Exodus 2:10)

משה

Implicit Value = 40 + 300 + 5 = 345

$$3 + 4 + 5 = 12$$

$$1 + 2 = 3$$

The association with Jesus that is so common with the number *three* is just as common with the implicit value of *three*:

… Jesus, the name given Him by the angel … (Luke 2:21)

Ιησους το κληθεν υπο αγγελου

Implicit Value = 10 + 8 + 200 + 70 + 400 + 200 + 300 + 70 + 20 + 30 + 8 + 9 + 5 + 50 + 400 + 80 + 70 + 1 + 3 + 3 + 5 + 30 + 70 + 400 = 2442

$$2 + 4 + 4 + 2 = 12$$

$$1 + 2 = 3$$

… Mary (Luke 1:27)

Μαριαμ

Implicit Value = 40 + 1 + 100 + 10 + 1 + 40 = 192

$$1 + 9 + 2 = 12$$

$$1 + 2 = 3$$

… she gave birth to her first child, a son. (Luke 2:7)

ετεκεν υιον πρωτοτοκον

Implicit Value = 5 + 300 + 5 + 20 + 5 + 50 + 400 + 10 + 70 + 50 + 80 + 100 + 800 + 300 + 70 + 300 + 70 + 20 + 70 + 50 = 2775

2 + 7 + 7 + 5 = 21

2 + 1 = 3

… for we have seen His star in far-off eastern lands, and have come to worship him. (Matthew 2:2)

εἰδομεν γαρ αυτου αστερα εν τη ανατολη και ηλθομεν προσκυνησαι αυτω

Implicit Value = 5 + 10 + 4 + 70 + 40 + 5 + 50 + 3 + 1 + 100 + 1 + 400 + 300 + 70 + 400 + 1 + 200 + 300 + 5 + 100 + 1 + 5 + 50 + 300 + 8 + 1 + 50 + 1 + 300 + 70 + 30 + 8 + 20 + 1 + 10 + 8 + 30 + 9 + 70 + 40 + 5 + 50 + 80 + 100 + 70 + 200 + 20 + 400 + 50 + 8 + 200 + 1 + 10 + 1 + 400 + 300 + 800 = 5772

5 + 7 + 7 + 2 = 21

2 + 1 = 3

… This is my much-loved Son; I am well pleased with Him. (2 Peter 1:17)

ο υιος αγαπητος μου εις ον εγω ευδοκησα

Implicit Value = 70 + 400 + 10 + 70 + 200 + 1 + 3 + 1 + 80 + 8 + 300 + 70 + 200 + 40 + 70 + 400 + 5 + 10 + 200 + 70 + 50 + 5 + 3 + 800 + 5 + 400 + 4 + 70 + 20 + 8 + 200 + 1 = 3774

3 + 7 + 7 + 4 = 21

2 + 1 = 3

… resurrection … (Acts 2:31)

αναστασεως

Implicit Value = 1 + 50 + 1 + 200 + 300 + 1 + 200 + 5 + 800 + 200 = 1758

1 + 7 + 5 + 8 = 21

2 + 1 = 3

Then the peoples of the earth shall see the Son of Man coming in a cloud with power ... (Luke 21:27)

οψονται υιον του ανθρωπου ερχομενον εν νεφελη μετα δυναμεως

Implicit Value = 70 + 700 + 70 + 50 + 300 + 1 + 10 + 400 + 10 + 70 + 50 + 300 + 70 + 400 + 1 + 50 + 9 + 100 + 800 + 80 + 70 + 400 + 5 + 100 + 600 + 70 + 40 + 5 + 50 + 70 + 50 + 5 + 50 + 50 + 5 + 500 + 5 + 30 + 8 + 40 + 5 + 300 + 1 + 4 + 400 + 50 + 1 + 40 + 5 + 800 + 200 = 7500

7 + 5 + 0 + 0 = 12

1 + 2 = 3

Jesus told the Samaritan woman that people soon became thirsty again after drinking the water from the well but not after drinking the water he gave them:

... water I will give ... (John 4:14)

υδωρ δωσω

Implicit Value = 400 + 4 + 800 + 100 + 4 + 800 + 200 + 800 = 3108

3 + 1 + 0 + 8 = 12

1 + 2 = 3

The Implicit Value 111

In the earlier chapter on the number *one*, I discussed the miraculous association that implicit values that were multiples of the number 37 had with Jesus. Another significant foundation number is 111. Examine the number 111 closely. It is the product of multiplying the number 37 times *three*, an act of God. It is also the number *one*, *three* times—that is, the number associated with God *three* times—symbolizing *three* divine entities unified into a single being, otherwise known as the Holy Trinity.

Many of the implicit values cited in previous sections are multiples of 111. Here are a few more examples:

… Jesus is the Son of God … (1 John 4:15)

οτι Ιησους εστιν υιος Θεου

Implicit Value = 70 + 300 + 10 + 10 + 8 + 200 + 70 + 400 + 200 + 5 + 200 + 300 + 10 + 50 + 400 + 10 + 70 + 200 + 9 + 5 + 70 + 400 = 2997

2997 = *111* * 27

… Nazarene … (Luke 4:34)

ναζαρηνε

Implicit Value = 50 + 1 + 7 + 1 + 100 + 8 + 50 + 5 = 222

222 = *111* * 2

… the King of Israel … (John 12:13)

και Βασιλευς του Ισραηλ

Implicit Value = 20 + 1 + 10 + 2 + 1 + 200 + 10 + 30 + 5 +
400 + 200 + 300 + 70 + 400 + 10 + 200 + 100 + 1 + 8 + 30 =
1998

1998 = *111* * 18

Eternal life is in Him, and this life gives light to all mankind.
(John 1:4)

εν αυτω ζωη ην και η ζωη ην φως των ανθρωπων

Implicit Value = 5 + 50 + 1 + 400 + 300 + 800 + 7 + 800 + 8
+ 8 + 50 + 20 + 1 + 10 + 8 + 7 + 800 + 8 + 8 + 50 + 500 + 800
+ 200 + 300 + 800 + 50 + 1 + 50 + 9 + 100 + 800 + 80 + 800
+ 50 = 7881

7881 = *111* * 71

… the Alpha and the Omega, the Beginning and the End, the
First and Last. (The Revelation 22:13)

αλφα και ω πρωτος και ο εσχατος αρχη και το τελος

Implicit Value = 1 + 30 + 500 + 1 + 20 + 1 + 10 + 800 + 80
+ 100 + 800 + 300 + 70 + 200 + 20 + 1 + 10 + 70 + 5 + 200 +
600 + 1 + 300 + 70 + 200 + 1 + 100 + 600 + 8 + 20 + 1 + 10 +
300 + 70 + 300 + 5 + 30 + 70 + 200 = 6105

6105 = *111* * 55

Summary

As I build the numeric code, number by number, the wonder of this
system becomes ever greater. The number *three* is a good example of
how the numbers in the numeric code extrapolate from the previous
numbers to achieve a new symbolism. The number *three*, being the

sum of the number *one* (associated with God) and the number *two* (opposites in flesh and spirit) results in a number associated with the Holy Trinity and their actions. The most miraculous of these actions was when God sent his Son to earth to sacrifice himself so that everyone might find salvation from sin associated with the Law.

Review the symbolism of the number *three*:

- The Holy Trinity

- Acts of God—especially involving Jesus or the Holy Spirit

- Age to begin God's service

- Association with Jesus

- Path to salvation

- God's chosen from the masses (demonstrated through the number twelve)

In this chapter, I also continued to build on the implicit values that I began in the chapter on the number *one*. In that chapter, I explained the implicit value of 37 which symbolizes the perfect act of God in sending his Son, Jesus, to earth. Now I have multiplied the implicit value of 37 by *three* to get the implicit value of 111 which symbolizes the Holy Trinity. I will continue this chain in later chapters.

The frequency of occurrence of the number *three* also builds the evidence that God is the author of this Biblical numeric code and therefore the Bible. When you see so many examples compressed together in a few pages, you have to wonder how anyone could fail to notice the symbolism. Yet the number *three* appears many more times than what I have shown in this chapter. Occurring over and over from book to book and writer to writer, there is no way the repeated use of this number in the same context with the same symbolism could be random.

As you know, there are *nine* numbers in the numeric code of the Bible. These *nine* numbers can logically be divided into *three* sets of *three* numbers. The number *three* is the last number in the first set. I will refer to this first set as the *spiritual numbers* because of their association with God and the Holy Trinity. From this point, I enter the *physical numbers*.

Four

Physical World

As I said earlier, the number *three* is the last of the spiritual numbers. The number *four* builds on the number *three* by adding physical form, thereby introducing the physical numbers. It symbolizes all that is physical about God's created works. Representations of the physical (carnal) world associated with the number *four* are all around. There are *four* elements (air, earth, fire, and water), *four* seasons, and *four* points to the compass. In Genesis, *four* rivers watered the Garden of Eden. The *fourth* commandment is the first commandment to refer to earthly matters. The number *four* appears even when the writers of the Bible describe the physical form of God. In the first chapter of the book of Ezekiel, the prophet sees a vision of *four* creatures who provide form to the presence of God. These same *four* creatures also appear in the book of The Revelation:

One day in June, when I was *thirty* years old, the heavens were suddenly opened to me and I saw visions from God. I saw, in this vision, a great storm coming toward me from the north, driving before it a huge cloud glowing with fire, with a mass of fire inside that flashed continually; and in the fire there was something that shone like polished brass.

Then from the center of the cloud, *four* strange forms appeared that looked like men, except that each had *four* faces and *two pair* of wings! Their legs were like those of men, but there feet were cloven like calves' feet, and shone like burnished brass. And beneath each of their wings I could see human hands.

The *four* living beings were joined wing to wing, and they flew straight forward without turning. Each had a face of a man in front, with a lion's face on the right side of his head, and the face of an ox on the left side, and the face of an eagle at the back of his head! Each had *two pairs* of wings spreading out from the middle of his back. One pair stretched out to attach to the wings of the living beings on each side, and the other pair covered his body. Wherever their spirit went they went, going straight forward without turning. (Ezekiel 1:3-12)

Lightening and thunder issued from the throne, and there were voices in the thunder. Directly in front of His throne were *seven* lighted lamps representing the *seven*-fold Spirit of God. Spread out before it was a shiny crystal sea. *Four* Living Beings, dotted front and back with eyes, stood at the throne's *four* sides. The first of these Living Beings was in the form of a lion; the second looked like an ox, the third had the face of a man; and the *fourth*, the form of an eagle, with wings spread out as though in flight. (The Revelation 4:5-7)

What can you make of these visions? The *four* creatures are symbols. The lion symbolizes kingship; the ox, a servant; the man, perfect humanity; and the eagle, deity. As amazing as it is that these same *four* creatures appear in both Ezekiel and The Revelation, they also relate to the *four* gospels—Matthew, Mark, Luke, and John. These *four* aspects of God are the themes, in the same order, of the gospels as they relate to Jesus. Matthew presents Jesus as the Messiah, the King of the Jews. Mark presents Jesus as the servant of God for man. The theme of Luke is Jesus' perfect humanity; whereas, John presents Christ as the divine Son of God.

In addition to physical form, the number *four* also relates to punishment, worldly service, and physical tests. Daniel prophesied the *four* worldly kingdoms of Babylon, Media-Persia, Greece, and Rome. Jesus only received 39 lashes (3 + 9 = 12; 1 + 2 = 3), because 40 (4 + 0 = 4) lashes would bring death. The Revelation speaks of *four* horsemen symbolizing the antichrist, war, famine, and death. Moses left Egypt at 40 years of age, began his ministry at 80 (8 + 0 = 8), and served for 40 years. The Bible has many references to the number *four*, and always the context is the same.

Physical Aspects of God

To look on God is to invite death. When Moses encountered the burning bush in the *third* chapter of Exodus, he covered his eyes because he was afraid to look upon God. Yet whenever the physical aspects of God are described from visions, the number *four* is there. As described above, the prophet Ezekiel experiences a vision of *four* living beings, each with *four* faces. They rode on *four* wheels constructed such that they could travel in any of the *four* directions. Why is the number *four* used so often in this context? Why not use six or eight or even three? When the physical nature of God is described, the divine numeric code calls for the number *four* and no other number.

Here is yet another example of a vision of God's form as *four* beings who bring judgment down on the world:

> Then I looked up again and saw *four* chariots coming from between what looked like *two* mountains made of brass. The first chariot was pulled by red horses, the second by black ones, the third by white horses, the *fourth* by dappled grays.
> "And what are these, sir?" I asked the angel.
> He replied, "These are the *four* heavenly spirits who stand before the Lord of all the heavens; they are going out to do His work." (Zechariah 6:1-5)

Four soldiers crucified Jesus, and his worldly possessions were divided into *four* piles:

> When the soldiers had crucified Jesus, they put His garments into *four* piles, one for each of them. (John 19:23)

Jesus was on earth in physical form 40 (4 + 0 = *4)* days after his crucifixion:

> During the *forty* days after His crucifixion He appeared to the apostles from time to time, actually alive, and proved to them

in many ways that it was really He Himself they were seeing. (Acts 1:3)

Physical Tests

When the Bible refers to physical tests, the number *four* and its other equivalent numbers are used. Some of the most famous stories from the Bible involve physical tests for God's chosen. You have likely heard these stories since your youth, but how many of you noticed the repeated message of the number *four*?

Daniel, Shadrach, Meshack, and Abednego withstood a physical test involving their diet. The number 10 (1 + 0 = *1*) also appears since the act of these *four* youths was associated with God:

> Well, at the end of the *ten* days, Daniel and his three friends looked healthier and better nourished than the youths who had been eating the food supplied by the king! So after that the steward fed them only vegetables and water, without the rich foods and wines!
>
> God gave the *four* youths great ability to learn and they soon mastered all the literature and science of the time. (Daniel 1:15-17)

Moses spent 40 days and 40 nights on Mt. Sinai.

> And Moses disappeared into the cloud-covered mountain top and was there for *forty* days and *forty* nights. (Exodus 24:18)

Jesus spent the same period being tempted in the wilderness.

> Then Jesus was led out into the wilderness by the Holy Spirit, to be tempted there by Satan. For *forty* days and *forty* nights, he ate nothing and became very hungry. (Matthew 4:1-2)

Lazarus lay in the tomb for *four* days to perhaps provide Jesus' greatest physical test. This period of time, of course, is different than the *three* days in the grave associated with Jesus:

> When they arrived at Bethany, they were told that Lazarus had already been in his tomb *four* days. (John 11:17)

Punishment on the World or the Chosen People

Whenever God is punishing his creation for sin or the evil of mankind, the action involves the number *four* or its equivalents.

The great flood in Noah's time resulted from rains that lasted 40 days:

> For *forty* days the roaring floods prevailed, covering the ground and lifting the boat high above the earth. (Genesis 7:17)

God's curse on the Israeli's for their faithlessness lasted 40 years:

> You must wander in the desert like nomads for *forty* years. In this way you will pay for your faithlessness, until the last of you lies dead in the desert.
> Since the spies were in the land for *forty* days, you must wander in the wilderness for *forty* years—a year for each day, bearing the burden of your sins. (Numbers 14:33-34)

A later punishment lasted the same period of time:

> Once again Israel sinned by worshipping other gods, so the Lord let them be conquered by the Philistines, who kept them in subjection for *forty* years. (Judges 13:1)

The same sin of idol worship led to other punishments:

> I will appoint over them *four* kinds of destroyers, says the Lord—the sword to kill, the dogs to tear, and the vultures and wild animals to finish up what's left. (Jeremiah 15:3)

> And the Lord says: *Four* great punishments await Jerusalem to destroy all life: war, famine, ferocious beasts, plague. (Ezekiel 14:21)

Demons punish mankind at the end of time:

> "Release the *four* mighty demons held bound at the River Euphrates." They had been kept in readiness for that year and month and day and hour, and now they were turned loose to kill a *third* of all mankind. (The Revelation 9:14-15)

The Entire World

It is highly likely the *four* rivers referenced in the Garden of Eden scripture symbolize the entire world known to the Hebrews at the time of Moses:

> A river from the land of Eden flowed through the garden to water it; afterwards the river divided into *four* branches.
> One of these was named the Pihon; it winds across the entire length of the land of Havilah, where nuggets of pure gold are found, also beautiful bdellium and even lapis lazuli. The second branch is called the Gihon, crossing the entire length of the land of Cush. The third branch is the Tigris, which flows to the east of the city of Asher. And the *fourth* is the Euphrates. (Genesis 2:10-14)

Please note that the rivers come from *one* source and then part into *four* named rivers. The **one** source you now know to represent the *one* God from which all physical life sprang. The *four* rivers then symbolize the entire physical world he created and gave to man.

Likewise, Paul's *four* missionary journeys symbolize the spread of the gospel to the entire world. In the book of Acts, the Holy Spirit calls Paul to spread the gospel on *four* missionary journeys. These *four* journeys established many early Christian churches that became the cradle of first century Christianity. Perhaps even more significantly, Paul used these journeys to spread the story of Christ beyond the Jews to the Gentiles (the other sheep in Jesus' flock described in John 10:16):

First Journey	Second Journey	Third Journey	*Fourth* Journey
Antioch (Syria)	Jerusalem	Antioch (Syria)	Jerusalem
Seleucia Pieria	Antioch (Syria)	Tarsus (Cilicia)	Caesarea
Salamis (Cyprus)	Tarsus (Cilicia)	Derbe (Lycaonia)	Tyre
Paphos (Cyprus)	Derbe (Lycaonia)	Lystra (Lycaonia)	Sidon
Perga (Pamphylia)	Lystra (Lycaonia)	Iconium	Myra
Antioch (Pisidia)	Iconium	Antioch (Pisidia)	Cnidus
Iconium	Antioch (Pisidia)	Galatia	Fair Havens (Lasea Crete)
Lystra (Lycaonia)	Dorylaeum	Ephesus	Malta
Derbe (Lycaonia)	Troas	Troas	Syracuse (Sicily)
Attalia (Pamphylia)	Neapolis-Kavala	Neapolis-Kavala	Rhegium
	Philippi	Philippi	Puteoli
	Amphipolis	Berea	Rome
	Appollonia	Corinth	
	Thessalonica	Assos	
	Beroea	Miletus	
	Athens	Patara	

Corinth	Tyre
Cenchreae	Caesarea
Ephesus	Jerusalem
Caesarea	

The last days will impact the entire world:

> Then I saw *four* angels standing at the *four* corners of the earth, holding back the *four* winds from blowing, so that not a leaf rustled in the trees, and the ocean became as smooth as glass. (The Revelation 7:1)

At Jesus' second coming the angels will gather his followers from the entire world:

> And I shall send forth my angels with the sound of a mighty trumpet blast, and they shall gather my chosen ones from the *four* winds, from one end of heaven to the other. (Matthew 24:31)

Worldly Kingdoms

Daniel was one of the great prophets of the Old Testament. What makes Daniel especially pertinent to the subject of this book is that Daniel gave time periods for when many of his prophecies would come true, and time periods can be converted into numbers. I will discuss more of Daniel's prophecies later. The relevant prophecy to this chapter is his famous prophecy of the great world kingdoms—first Babylon, then Media-Persia, then Greece, and finally Rome:

> In my dream I saw a great storm on a mighty ocean, with strong winds blowing from every direction. Then *four* huge animals came up out of the water, each different from the other. The first was like a lion, but it had eagle's wings! And as I watched, its wings were pulled off so that it could no longer

fly, and it was left standing on the ground, on *two* feet, like a man; and a man's mind was given to it. The second animal looked like a bear with its paw raised, ready to strike. It held *three* ribs between its teeth, and I heard a voice saying to it, "Get up! Devour many people!" The third of these strange animals looked like a leopard, but on its back it had wings like those of birds, and it had *four* heads! And great power was given to it over all mankind.

Then, as I watched in my dream, a *fourth* animal rose up out of the ocean, too dreadful to describe and incredibly strong. It devoured some of its victims by tearing them apart with its huge iron teeth, and others it crushed beneath its feet …

… "These *four* huge animals," he said, "represent *four* kings who will someday rule the earth. But in the end, the people of the Most High God shall rule the governments of the world forever and forever." (Daniel 7:2-7, 17)

After prophesying the defeat of the Persians by the Greeks, Daniel predicts the division of the Greek empire into *four* pieces—Macedonia, Syria, Egypt, and Asia Minor:

… the shaggy-haired goat is the nation of Greece, and its long horn represents the first great king of that country. When you saw the horn break off, and *four* smaller horns replace it, this meant that the Grecian Empire will break into *four* sections with *four* kings, none of them as great as the first. (Daniel 8:21-22)

Worldly Service

Earlier, you saw 30 (3 + 0 = 3) as the age usually quoted in scripture for a servant of the Lord to begin God's service. Now in the following scriptures, you see how a term of 40 (4 + 0 = 4) years is used to express the length of worldly service. I have already referenced Moses' term of 40 years in the text above. Combining Moses with the names of the kings listed below, you get a notable group indeed.

Saul reigned as king of Israel for 40 years:

> Then the people begged for a king, and God gave them Saul (son of Kish), a man of the tribe of Benjamin, who reigned for *forty* years. (Acts 13:21)

David reigned for the same period:

> So David made a contract before the Lord with the leaders of Israel there at Hebron, and they crowned him king of Israel. He had already been the king of Judah for *seven* years, since the age of *thirty*. He then ruled thirty-three years in Jerusalem as king of both Israel and Judah; so he reigned for *forty* years altogether. (2 Samuel 5:3-5)

As did David's son Solomon:

> He ruled in Jerusalem for *forty* years. (1 Kings 11:42)

Implicit Values

Similar to the above examples where the number *four* appears explicitly in the scriptures, the implicit uses of the number carry the same symbolism. Scriptures describing the physical aspects of God, physical tests, punishments, and worldly service result in an implicit value of *four*. A few examples are provided below:

> … Joshua … (Joshua 1:1)
> or Yehoshua, is the Hebrew equivalent of the Greek name Jesus, though it was most often shortened to Yeshua by the time of Jesus

יהושע

Implicit Value = 10 + 5 + 6 + 300 + 70 = 391

$3 + 9 + 1 = 13$

$1 + 3 = \textbf{4}$

... this Temple ... (John 2:20)

ο ναος

Implicit Value = $70 + 50 + 1 + 70 + 200 = 391$

$3 + 9 + 1 = 13$

$1 + 3 = \textbf{4}$

... the Life (John 14:6)

η ζωη

Implicit Value = $8 + 7 + 800 + 8 = 823$

$8 + 2 + 3 = 13$

$1 + 3 = \textbf{4}$

You saw the Greek spelling of love earlier. Here is the Hebrew spelling:

... love (Genesis 22:2)

אהבה

Implicit Value = $1 + 5 + 2 + 5 = 13$

$1 + 3 = \textbf{4}$

Amazingly, the implicit value of the Hebrew name of God that refers to his almighty strength and power, physical attributes of God, carries the same symbolism:

El (Almighty God)

אל

Implicit Value = 31

$3 + 1 = 4$

Finally, when you multiply the foundation number of 111 by *four*, you get the value for Damascus which was founded approximately 2500 BCE and is the oldest continuously inhabited city in the world:

… Damascus (Genesis 14:15)

דמשק

Implicit Value = 4 + 40 + 300 + 100 = **444**

444 = 111 * 4

Summary

With this chapter, I have explored the number *four*, which represents the physical world, the creation of God. Again, the numbers in the divine numeric code build on the preceding numbers. In the previous chapter, you learned that the number *three* is the last of the spiritual numbers. Adding a dimension, you now enter the realm of the physical, first symbolized by the number *four*. If the number *three* is used in relation to acts of God, it only makes sense that the number *four* should represent the physical universe that he created.

Remember, the message of the number *four* is significant enough to apply to the physical form of God. Revisit in summary fashion the symbolism of the number *four*:

- Physical aspects of God

- Physical tests

- Punishment

- Entire world

- Worldly kingdoms

- Worldly service

I am nearly halfway through an exploration of the divine numeric code. By now, it is obvious that the use of these numbers in the Bible, along with their assigned symbolism, cannot be random. The simple, logical design of the numeric code implies a very high order of intelligence. Then when you consider the number of writers involved over the centuries, you must get a sense of the required omnipotence and omnipresence, as well as the lack of any restriction of time on the author.

Five

Physical Body

With the number *four*, I evaluated the first of the physical numbers. Continuing the progression, the number *five* adds yet another dimension. Whereas the number *four* represents the entire world of physical creation, the number *five* represents the result of the physical world acting on the individual. It symbolizes the body, the senses, injury, and temptation. It also has a tie to nature and to overcoming physical constraints.

Everyone who has read much of the Bible has noticed the more common numbers like *three* and *seven*. Even if you did not realize the symbolic meaning within them, you would have to notice the repetition of their occurrences. But do you remember the number *five* occurring in the Bible? Perhaps you remember that Jesus had *five* wounds on the cross, or that one of his most famous miracles was the feeding of the 5000 (5 + 0 + 0 + 0 = 5). Or perhaps not—*five* is not one of the more commonly used numbers in the Bible. Yet, it is in the study of the less common numbers, such as the number *five*, that you see the true miracle of the numeric code of the Bible.

The number *five* occurs explicitly in the Bible often enough to discern its meaning without question. Even if it did not, there are many other references to the number *five*. For example, each person has *five* fingers and *five* senses. There is also the Law, which represents a bridge between God's realm in heaven and the physical life of man. As you saw previously, the Law is composed of 613 (6 + 1 + 3 = 10, 1 + 0 = *1*) commandments, or mitzvot. Amazingly, the 613 mitzvot are made up of 248 (2 + 4 + 8 = 14, 1 + 4 = 5) positive commandments and 365 (3 + 6 + 5 = 14, 1 + 4 = 5) negative commandments. 248 at the time was believed to be the number of bones and significant organs in the human body, and 365 corresponds to the number of days in a year.

Senses and Physical Desires

With the *five* senses of the human body as a guide, it is extremely logical that the number *five* would apply to urges related to the senses. In addition, instinctual urges, such as the sex drive, fit within this category. From Mosaic Law to David and Bathsheba, to the Letters of Paul, the Bible preaches control of these urges. Why is this control so important? Because letting these urges control you leads to sin, and sin leads to spiritual death and separation from God.

But why would the number *five* appear so consistently throughout the Bible in relation to the senses and physical desires unless it was part of a master plan? Old Testament and New Testament writers use the number *five* in the same way. When you see the following scriptures, you will have to pause in amazement at the miracle of God's word.

To satisfy his desire for Rachel, Jacob had to work 14 (1 + 4 = 5) years made up of *two seven*-year terms.

> So Jacob spent the next *seven* years working to pay for Rachel. But they seemed to him but a few days, he was so much in love. Finally the time came for him to marry her.
>
> "I have fulfilled my contract," Jacob said to Laban. "Now give me my wife, so that I can sleep with her."
>
> So Laban invited all the men of the settlement to celebrate with Jacob at a big party. Afterwards, that night, when it was dark, Laban took Leah to Jacob, and he slept with her.... But in the morning it was Leah!
>
> "What sort of trick is this?" Jacob raged at Laban. "I worked for *seven* years for Rachel. What do you mean by this trickery?"
>
> "It's not our custom to marry off a younger daughter ahead of her sister," Laban replied smoothly. "Wait until the bridal week is over and you can have Rachel too—if you promise to work for me another *seven* years!"
>
> So Jacob agreed to work *seven* more years. Then Laban gave him Rachel too. (Genesis 29:20-28)

Joseph gave advice to Pharaoh concerning the famine that was to follow the years of plenty (total of 14 years):

> Let Pharaoh divide Egypt into *five* administrative districts, and let the officials of these districts gather into the royal storehouses all the excess crops of the next *seven* years so there will be enough to eat when the *seven* years of famine come. (Genesis 41:34-35)

When discovered in Egypt, Joseph prepared a feast for his brothers, giving more food to his favorite:

> Their food was served to them from his own table. He gave the largest serving to Benjamin—*five* times as much as to any of the others! (Genesis 43:34)

When running from Saul, David was hungry and asked for food:

> Now, what is there to eat? Give me *five* loaves of bread, or anything else you can. (1 Samuel 21:3)

The Samaritan woman's lust was demonstrated by the number of her marriages:

> "But I'm not married," the woman replied.
> "All too true!" Jesus said. "For you have had *five* husbands, and you aren't even married to the man you're living with now." (John 4:17-18)

Look at the number of people who died for sexual improprieties:

> Another lesson for us is what happened when some of them sinned with other men's wives, and *twenty-three thousand* fell dead in *one* day. And don't try the Lord's patience—they did, and died from snake bites. (1 Corinthians 10:8-10)
> $(2 + 3 + 0 + 0 + 0 = 5)$

And, of course, there was the feeding of the 5000 (5 + 0 + 0 + 0 = 5):

> Late in the afternoon His disciples came to Him and said, "Tell all the people to go away to the nearby villages and farms and buy themselves some food, for there is nothing to eat here in this desolate spot, and it is getting late."
>
> But Jesus said, "You feed them."
>
> "With what?" they asked. It would take a fortune to buy food for all this crowd!"
>
> "How much food do we have?" He asked. "Go and find out."
>
> They came back to report that there were *five* loaves and *two* fish.
>
> Then Jesus told the crowd to sit down, and soon colorful groups of *fifty* or a *hundred* each were sitting on the green grass.
>
> He took the *five* loaves and *two* fish and looking up to heaven, gave thanks for the food. Breaking the loaves into pieces, He gave some of the bread and fish to each disciple to place before the people. And the crowd ate until they could hold no more!
>
> There were about *5000* men there for that meal, and afterwards *twelve* basketfuls of scraps were picked up off the grass! (Mark 6:35-44)

Miracles

With the feeding of the 5000 as an introduction, you can carry the concept forward to miracles in general. Repeatedly you have seen how the numbers in the code build upon one another. *Four* (the world) gives way to *five* (the body) and the physical tests associated with the number *four* give way to the overcoming the physical constraints. There are 32 (3 + 2 = 5) miracles of Jesus recorded in the Gospels. 24 (2 + 4 = *6*) of these miracles are performed on people, and *eight* of the miracles are performed on nature. When you get to the chapters on the numbers *six* and *eight*, you will discover just how appropriate these divisions are.

Miracles Performed on People	Matthew	Mark	Luke	John
Healing of Demoniac in Capernaum		1:21-28	4:31-34	
Healing of Peter's Mother-in-Law	8:14-15	1:29-31	4:38-39	
Cleansing of Leper	8:1-4	1:40-45	5:12-16	
Healing of the Paralytic	9:1-8	2:1-12	5:17-26	
Healing the Withered Hand	12:9-14	3:1-6	6:6-11	
Gadarene Demoniac	8:28-34	5:1-20	8:26-39	
Woman with Hemorrhage	9:18-26	5:21-43	8:40-56	
Raising Jairus' Daughter	9:18-26	5:21-43	8:40-56	
Canaanite Woman	15:21-28	7:24-30		
Healing of Deaf Man		7:31-37		
Healing of Blind Man in Bethsaida		8:22-26		
Healing of Possessed Boy	17:14-21	9:14-29	9:37-43	
Healing of Blind Man/Men	20:29-34	10:46-52	18:35-43	
Centurion of Capernaum	8:5-13		7:1-10	4:46-54
Healing of *Two* Blind Men	9:27-31			
Speechless Demoniac	9:32-34		11:14-15	
Healing of Blind/Mute Demoniac	12:22-30			
Raising of Widow's Son			7:11-17	
Healing of Crippled Woman			13:10-17	
Healing of Man with Dropsy			14:1-6	
Healing of Ten Lepers			17:11-19	
Healing at Bethesda Pool				5:2-47
Healing of Man Born Blind				9:1-41
Raising of Lazarus				11:1-44

Miracles Performed on Nature				
Stilling the Storm	8:23-27	4:35-41	8:22-25	
Feeding of *5000*	14:13-21	6:32-34	9:10-17	6:1-15
Walking on Water	14:22-33	6:45-52		6:16-21
Feeding of *4000*	15:32-39	8:1-10		
Cursing of Fig Tree	21:18-22	11:12-26		
Temple Tax Payment	17:24-27			
Fish Catch			5:1-11	
Marriage at Cana				2:1-11

Offspring and Generations

As you saw in the story of Jacob and Rachel, the number 14 (1 + 4 = 5) carries a symbolism associated with the result of physical union. This symbolism extends to offspring and generations.

Abraham was symbolically the appropriate age when Haggar gave him his first offspring, Ishmael, though he was not to be the patriarch of the chosen people:

> So Haggar gave Abram a son, and Abram named him Ishmael. Abram was *eighty-six* years old at this time. (Genesis 16:15-16)
> $$8 + 6 = 14$$
> $$1 + 4 = 5$$

Though Jacob had 12 sons from which come the 12 tribes of Israel, he had a total of 14 sons and grandsons through his beloved wife Rachel:

> Also in the total of Jacob's household were these *fourteen* sons and descendants of Jacob and Rachel … (Genesis 46:19-22)

When Matthew describes the genealogy from Abraham to Jesus Christ, the list contains *three* sections of 14 generations:

> So all the generations from Abraham to David are *fourteen*; and *fourteen* from King David's time to the exile; and *fourteen* from the exile to Christ. (Matthew 1:17)

Injury

Similar to the senses and physical urges, injuries to the body often have the number *five* associated with them. In the second book of Samuel, murder was often committed by stabbing with a knife or sword under the **fifth** rib. Joab, who committed multiple murders in this way, was himself murdered in the first book of Kings. But the number *five* does not only pertain to killing. All sorts of injuries have the symbolism of the number *five* in the scriptures. As referenced earlier, Jesus himself experienced *five* wounds on the cross.

Joshua's killing of the Amorite kings not only involved injury but symbolized subjection of the senses:

> With that, Joshua plunged his sword into each of the *five* kings, killing them. He then hanged them on *five* trees until evening. (Joshua 10:26)

Look at the description of Saul's grandson:

> There was a little lame grandson of King Saul named Mephibosheth, who was the son of Prince Jonathan. He was *five* years old at the time Saul and Jonathan were killed at the battle of Jezreel. When the news of the battle reached the capital, the child's nurse grabbed him and fled and dropped him as she was running, and he became lame. (2 Samuel 4:4)

When Israel's King Ahaziah lay injured, he sent for Elijah:

> Israel's new king, Ahaziah, had fallen off the upstairs porch of his palace at Samaria and was seriously injured …
> … It was Elijah the prophet!" the king exclaimed. Then he sent an army captain with *fifty* soldiers to arrest him. (2 Kings 1:2, 8-9)
> 5 + 0 = 5

The Philistines offered a guilt offering to relieve the plague set on them for capturing the Ark of God:

> "What guilt offering shall we send?" they asked.
> And they were told, "Send *five* gold models of the tumor caused by the plague, and *five* gold models of the rats that have ravaged the whole land." (1 Samuel 6:4-5)

David took *five* stones as weapons against Goliath, but he only required *one* stone to slay him because the feat was associated with God:

> Then he picked up *five* smooth stones from a stream and put them in his shepherd's bag and, armed only with his shepherd's staff and sling, started across to Goliath …
>
> … David shouted in reply, "You come to me with a sword and spear, but I come to you in the name of the Lord of the armies of heaven and of Israel—the very God you have defied …
>
> … As Goliath approached, David ran out to meet him and, reaching into his shepherd's bag, took out *a stone*, hurled it from his sling, and hit the Philistine in the forehead. The stone sank in, and the man fell on his face to the ground. (1 Samuel 17:40, 45, 48-49)

The rich man in torment for his sins wanted to send Lazarus with a message for his brothers:

> Then the rich man said, "O Father Abraham, then please send him to my father's home—for I have *five* brothers—to warn them about this place of torment lest they come here when they die." (Luke 16:27-28)

Look how many times Paul receive 40 minus one lashes:

> *Five* different times the Jews gave me their terrible *thirty-nine* lashes. (2 Corinthians 11:24)

At the end of time, people who do not serve God will suffer the pain of scorpion stings:

> Then locusts came from the smoke and descended onto the earth and were given power to sting like scorpions. They were told not to hurt the grass or plants or trees, but to attack those people who did not have the mark of God on their foreheads.

They were not to kill them, but to torture them for *five* months with agony like the pain of scorpion stings. In those days men will try to kill themselves but won't be able to—death will not come. (The Revelation 9:3-6)

Physical Appearances of Jesus Following Death and Resurrection

Jesus did not dematerialize in the tomb and transport to heaven as spirit. He rose from the dead and walked out of the tomb to spend time on earth with his followers. In fact, he went out of his way to prove the physicality of his body. He showed them his wounds; he ate with them; and he sat with them, giving them their final lessons on prophecy and what their mission was to be. The following is a list of scriptures in which Jesus physically appeared to his followers after he rose from the tomb:

1. John 20:10-18	To Mary Magdalene outside the tomb
2. Matthew 28:5-10	To the women running from the tomb
3. Luke 24:34 1 Corinthians 15:5	To Peter
4. Luke 24:13-31	To *two* disciples on the road to Emmaus
5. Luke 24:36-49 John 20:19-23	To his disciples except for Thomas
6. John 20:24-29	To his disciples with Thomas present
7. John 21:1-14	To *seven* of the disciples fishing in Galilee
8. 1 Corinthians 15:6	To more than *five hundred* of his followers

    9. 1 Corinthians 15:7   To his brother James

   10. Matthew 28:16-20   To the Eleven on a
                                       mountain in Galilee

   11. Mark 16:14-15   To the Eleven in Jerusalem

   12. Luke 24:44-49   Another meeting with the
        Acts 1:4-5   Eleven

   13. Acts 1:6   To the apostles who would
                                         be preaching

14. Acts 1:9   Ascension
       Luke 24:50-51

Implicit Values

Included here are a few examples of implicit values involving the number *five* and then I will move on to another interesting use of the number *five* that involves both an explicit use of the number and multiple implicit values of that number.

The act of creation brought physical form:

... created ... (Genesis 1:1)

ברא

Implicit Value = 2 + 200 + 1 = 203

2 + 0 + 3 = 5

Jesus also preached to ignore the faults of others and examine your own failings:

... someone else's eye ... (Luke 6:41)

τω οφθαλμω του αδελφου σου

Implicit Value = 300 + 800 + 70 + 500 + 9 + 1 + 30 + 40 + 800 + 300 + 70 + 400 + 1 + 4 + 5 + 30 + 500 + 70 + 400 + 200 + 70 + 400 = 5000

5 + 0 + 0 + 0 = *5*

The Number and Implicit Value—153

The twenty-first chapter of John contains a relatively well-known account of one of Jesus' appearances following his death and resurrection. Embedded in the story is a peculiar number, namely the number 153 (1 + 5 + 3 = **9**). First read the story and then think of the possible symbolism in the number 153.

Later Jesus appeared again to the disciples beside the Lake of Galilee. This is how it happened:

A group of us were there—Simon Peter, Thomas, "The Twin," Nathanael from Cana in Galilee, my brother James and I and *two* other disciples.

Simon Peter said, "I'm going fishing."

"We'll come too," we all said. We did, but caught nothing all night. At dawn we saw a man standing on the beach but couldn't see who he was.

He called, "Any fish, boys?"

"No," we replied.

Then he said, "Throw out your net on the right-hand side of the boat, and you'll get plenty of them!" So we did, and couldn't draw in the net because of the weight of the fish, there were so many!

Then I said to Peter, "It is the Lord!" At that, Simon Peter put on his tunic (for he was stripped to the waist) and jumped into the water and swam ashore. The rest of us stayed in the boat and pulled the loaded net to the beach about *300* feet away. When we got there, we saw that a fire was kindled and fish were frying over it, and there was bread.

"Bring some of the fish you've just caught," Jesus said. So Simon Peter went out and dragged the net ashore. By his count there were **153** large fish; and yet the net hadn't torn. (John 21:1-11)

Why in this story is the number 153 so exact? Earlier in the account, John uses an approximation for the distance from shore, saying it was "about **300** feet" (3 + 0 + 0 = 3). John used the number **300** because this was an act of God associated with Jesus. But why then did he use the number 153? Would not another approximation, such as "about 150 large fish" done just as well?

You should recognize by now that a number this significant is not placed accidentally. Examine the number more closely. It is composed of a single *one*, a single *five*, and a single *three*. If you add the digits together, you get the number *nine*. I discuss the number *nine* in a later chapter, but as a preview just equate the number *nine* with the end of time.

The number *one* refers to God. The number *five* refers to the physical body. And the number *three* relates to acts of God, with a special association with Jesus. You put the three numbers and their total together, and you get a number that refers to God sending his son to conquer death's power over the body. If you accept God's invitation, then at the end of time (*nine*) you will live forever in the presence of the Lord.

The significance and power of this number buried in a story from the Book of John is tremendous. It is like a diamond buried in the rock. But it only appears explicitly one time. What other proof do you have of its significance? Del Washburn in *Theomatics* found a pattern involving the number 153. I have already examined the concept of multiples of implicit values in two other chapters. In those chapters, I looked at multiples of the values 37 and 111. Del Washburn found a similar pattern of multiples involving the number 153.

The first examples link to the fishing theme of the 21st chapter of John (the story related in the first part of this section). In this story, the *sea* is commonly thought to symbolize mankind, the *net* to symbolize the kingdom of God, and the *fish* to symbolize the saved. The last two implicit value examples refer to salvation.

... casting a net into the sea ... (Matthew 4:18)

βαλλοντας αμφιβλητρον εις την θαλασσαν

Implicit Value = 2 + 1 + 30 + 30 + 70 + 50 + 300 + 1 + 200
+ 1 + 40 + 500 + 10 + 2 + 30 + 8 + 200 + 300 + 100 + 70 + 50
+ 5 + 10 + 200 + 300 + 8 + 50 + 9 + 1 + 30 + 1 + 200 + 200 +
1 + 50 = 3060

3060 = *153* * 20

... the net (John 21:11)

το δικτυον

Implicit Value = 300 + 70 + 4 + 10 + 20 + 300 + 400 + 70 +
50 = 1224

1224 = *153* * 8

... fishes ... (Luke 9:13)

ιχθυες

Implicit Value = 10 + 600 + 9 + 400 + 5 + 200 = 124

1224 = *153* * 8

... the door ... (Luke 13:25)

την θυραν

Implicit Value = 300 + 8 + 50 + 9 + 400 + 100 + 1 + 50 =
918

918 = *153* * 6

… the narrow gate (Matthew 7:13)

της στενης πυλης

Implicit Value = 300 + 8 + 200 + 200 + 300 + 5 + 50 + 8 + 200 + 80 + 400 + 30 + 8 + 200 = 1989

1989 = *153* * 13

Summary

After reviewing the three spiritual numbers—*one, two,* and *three*—you have just completed a review of the second of three physical numbers. The number *five* narrows the symbolism down from the physical world (represented by the number *four*) to the physical body and the result of the world acting on the body. Scriptures including the number *five* are associated with the following:

- The body

- The senses

- Physical desires

- Miracles

- Overcoming constraints of nature

- Offspring and generations

- Physical injury

- Physical appearance of Jesus following death and resurrection

Though not one of the more common numbers in the Bible, the number *five* offers some of the more tremendous evidence of the divine numeric code. The examples of its use that I have reviewed, offer glimpses into the symbolism God uses to relay his message. Then you have the rare and wonderful number 153 that requires you to use what you have learned about three distinct numbers (*one*, *five*, and *three*) and the yet unstudied number *nine*. It shows the power you will have to decipher God's message when you more fully understand the meaning of all of the numbers in the divine numeric code. For this apparently insignificant number holds the symbolism of the resurrection through salvation.

Six

Man

The number *six* has a bad reputation, and a lot of the examples in this chapter will reinforce that reputation. But as I have shown, there are no completely good or bad numbers, and the number *six* is no exception. When the symbolism associated with the number *six* is good, it is very good, and when it is bad, it is very bad. The number six gets its reputation because the most prevalent symbolism associated with it in the Bible is very bad.

Following the numbers *one, two*, and *three*—which are essentially spiritual in nature—the numbers *four, five*, and *six* are essentially physical in nature, with each number getting less spiritual and more carnal. Remember the definition of the word *carnal*—having characteristics of the physical world and giving in to the appetites of the flesh. Since you finally attain perfection with the number *seven*, the number *six* is left to represent the most carnal, and sometimes even evil, side of man that prevents him from attaining his goal of perfection. Symbolism associated with the number *six*, then, revolves around giving in to those appetites, or conquering them.

The number *six* does not appear in the Bible often as an explicit number, but it is nevertheless very significant. It is, fundamentally, the number of man. God created man on the *sixth* day. The *sixth* commandment prohibits the murder of man. Beginning with the physical world of the number *four*, the numeric code adds the concept of the individual to obtain the physical body in the number *five*. Then it adds the principle of the soul in the number *six*. Representing the longing for perfection inherent in every human being, the number *six* sometimes represents the best man can be but most often represents falling short of that perfection.

For this reason, Satan has a particular tie to the number *six*. It is Satan that tempts man and lays the traps that keep him from attaining perfection. It is Satan that battles God for the souls of men and does everything he can to separate man from God. If Satan has his way, the world represented by the number *six* would be a realm of sin and depravity with him as its ruler:

> How you are fallen from heaven, O Lucifer, son of the morning! How you are cut down to the ground—mighty though you were against the nations of the world. For you said to yourself, "I will ascend to heaven and rule the angels. I will preside on the Mount Assembly far away in the north. I will climb to the highest heavens and be like the Most High." But instead, you will be brought down to the pit of hell, down to the lowest depths. Everyone there will stare at you and ask, "Can this be the one who shook the earth and the kingdoms of the world? Can this be the one who destroyed the world and made it into a shambles and demolished its greatest cities and had no mercy on his prisoners?" (Isaiah 14:12-17)

Probably the peak of Satan's influence on the world came at the trial and execution of Jesus, the Son of God. Have you ever worked through the scriptures to count the number of trials Jesus experienced? As you now might expect, there were *six* trials, *three* religious trials under the Jewish legal system, and *three* civil trials under the Roman legal system:

Trials of Jesus Christ

1. Before Annas, the influential former high priest, who blessed sending him to Caiaphas

2. Before Caiaphas, the high priest, who pronounced a death sentence for blasphemy

3. Before the Sanhedrin, who approved the sentence

4. First appearance before Pontius Pilate who pronounced him not guilty and sent him to Herod Antipas

5. Before Herod Antipas, who pronounced him not guilty and returned him to Pilate

6. Second appearance before Pilate, who pronounced him not guilty but turned him over for execution

The Jewish trials did not follow Jewish law. Among the many violations were: there was never a formal accusation, and they ultimately convicted Jesus on his own testimony because they found no other valid evidence. But it was not the Jewish trials that ultimately sent Jesus to his death. Both Herod Antipas and Pontius Pilate were Roman citizens. According to the Bible, both of them knew him to be innocent. Pontius Pilate ultimately took the most political route and knowingly sentenced an innocent man to his death. Jesus was crucified under the worldly authority of the Roman government.

Imperfect Creation

In the first chapter of Genesis, God created man in his image, but as a portent of what was to come, this act of creation came on the *sixth* day. Man sinned in the Garden of Eden and by the *sixth* chapter of the Bible, God was planning the destruction of his creation. He saw that man was imperfect, wicked, and tending towards evil. It broke his heart.

The *six* days of creation that resulted in an imperfect man, led to man working *six* days of the week:

> *Six* days are for your daily duties and your regular work, but the *seventh* day is a day of Sabbath rest before the Lord your God. (Exodus 20:9-10)

Man became so evil that God decided to destroy him but selected Noah to save his creation:

> So Noah did everything the Lord commanded him. He was *six hundred* years old when the flood came. (Genesis 7:5-6)
> $6 + 0 + 0 = 6$

> And the water covered the earth *150* days. (Genesis 7:24)
> $1 + 5 + 0 = 6$

Angels

Based on their description, the seraphim and other angels identify more closely with man than with God. As you may know from the first chapter of Colossians, they too were created by God. They probably are not perfect and may have some freedom of will although under the sovereign control of God. After all, Lucifer, or Satan, was himself an angel. As shown earlier, his fall from grace after attempting to rule the angels is described in the fourteenth chapter of Isaiah. Satan apparently took *one third* of the angels with him. They are now referred to as fallen angels, or demons.

A description of the angels came in two visions:

> The year King Uzziah died I saw the Lord! He was sitting on a lofty throne, and the Temple was filled with His glory. Hovering about Him were mighty *six*-winged seraphs. With two of there wings they covered their faces; with two others they covered their feet; and with two they flew. (Isaiah 6:1-2)

> Each of these Living Beings has *six* wings, and the central sections of their wings were covered with eyes. (The Revelation 4:8)

Rule of Man

Kingdoms ruled by man fall short of the perfection of the Kingdom of God. This principle was a major subject of Jesus' teachings. Many of these kingdoms throughout history opposed the chosen people of God. They became associated with evil or Satan in the Bible. When a number appears in relation to these kingdoms, it is often the number *six*.

Pharaoh and Egypt were associated with carnal rule:

> So Pharaoh led the chase in his chariot, followed by the pick of Egypt's chariot corps—**600** chariots in all—and other chariots driven by Egyptian officers. (Exodus 14:6-7)

Note the number of troops associated with the kings of Midian and the number of troops slain as an act of God through Gideon:

> By this time King Zebah and King Zalmunna with a remnant of *fifteen thousand* troops were in Karkor. That was all that was left of the allied armies of the east; for *one hundred twenty thousand* had already been killed. (Judges 8:10)
> $$1 + 5 + 0 + 0 + 0 = 6$$
> $$1 + 2 + 0 + 0 + 0 + 0 = 3$$

Even the realm of King Solomon, who built the Temple, was still a kingdom ruled by man:

> He also made a huge ivory throne and overlaid it with gold. It had *six* steps … (1 Kings 10:18-19)

And even when that rule is just and to be rewarded, it is still the rule of man:

> It was just before this that Hezekiah became deathly sick and Isaiah the prophet (Amoz' son) went to visit him and gave him this message from the Lord.

"Set your affairs in order, for you are going to die; you will not recover from this illness."

When Hezekiah heard this, he turned his face to the wall and prayed:

"O Lord, don't you remember how true I've been to you and how I've always tried to obey you in everything you said?" Then he broke down with great sobs.

So the Lord sent another message to Isaiah:

Go and tell Hezekiah that the Lord God of your forefather David hears you praying and sees your tears and will let you live *fifteen* more years. (Isaiah 38:1-5)

The mark of the beast is a puzzle that I will solve in a later chapter. Look closely at the text. What further proof do you need that there is a divine use of numbers that add another dimension of understanding to the interpretation of biblical scripture? These scriptures contain an explicit reference to the numeric code of the Bible:

He required everyone—great and small, rich and poor, slave and free—to be tattooed with a certain mark on the right hand or on the forehead. And no one could get a job or even buy in any store without the permit of that mark, which was either the name of the Creature or the code number of his name. Here is a puzzle that calls for careful thought to solve it. Let those who are able, interpret this code: the numeric values of the letters in his name add to *666*! (The Revelation 13:16-18)

Implicit Values

The implicit values associated with the number *six* shout the wonder of the numeric code of the Bible. Association with Satan's influence and characteristics commonly identified with Satan repeatedly have implicit values that result in the number *six*. I will first examine the implicit values of some single words and short phrases. Then I will show examples of another multiple implicit value. I will share an amazing fact about the implicit value of the name Satan in Hebrew in a later chapter, but look at the value of the Satan in Greek:

... Satan ... (Matthew 3:23)

Σατανας

Implicit Value = 200 + 1 + 300 + 1 + 50 + 1 + 200 = 753

7 + 5 + 3 = 15

1 + 5 = **6**

Six also represents the implicit value of the carnal world:

... world ... (John 1:10)

κοσμος

Implicit Value = 20 + 70 + 200 + 40 + 70 + 200 = 600

6 + 0 + 0 = **6**

The implicit value for the word power and the phrase associated with Pontius Pilate are also equivalent:

Luke 21:27 ... power ... (Luke 21:27)

δυναμεως

Implicit Value = 4 + 400 + 50 + 1 + 40 + 5 + 800 + 200 = 1500

1 + 5 + 0 + 0 = **6**

... authority of the governor ... (Luke 20:19)

τη εξουσια ηγεμουος

Implicit Value = 300 + 8 + 5 + 60 + 70 + 400 + 200 + 10 + 1
+ 8 + 3 + 5 + 40 + 70 + 50 + 70 + 200 = 1500

$1 + 5 + 0 + 0 = 6$

The number *six* is often thought of as a bad number. But as I have said, all numbers have both negative and positive traits. In fact, Jesus, who came to earth as a man to experience death and then conquer it to offer salvation to mankind, shares the implicit value of *six*. I will address symbolism associated with the name of Jesus much more in a later chapter, but for now, I will just show the implicit value:

... Jesus ... (Mark 1:9)

Ιησους

Implicit Value = 10 + 8 + 200 + 70 + 400 + 200 = 888

$8 + 8 + 8 = 24$

$2 + 4 = 6$

And Jesus declares himself to be *the light of the world*.

... light ... (John 8:12)

φωσ

Implicit Value = 500 + 800 + 200 = 1500

$1 + 5 + 0 + 0 = 6$

The church in Antioch is where the followers of Jesus were first called Christians.

... church ... (Acts 11:26)

εκκλησια

Implicit Value = 5 + 20 + 20 + 30 + 8 + 200 + 10 + 1 = 294

2 + 9 + 4 = 15

1 + 5 = **6**

The Number and Implicit Value—276

Do you remember what you have learned about implicit values occurring in multiples? Sometimes certain implicit values appear in multiples in relation to the same topics as their explicit counterparts. I have previously cited examples of multiples of 37, 111, and 153. The unlikely multiple implicit value demonstrated and examined in this chapter is the value 276. This strange number appears explicitly in the twenty-seventh chapter of Acts. In this account, Paul was on his way to stand trial before Caesar. The ship on which his captors were transporting him was caught in a storm, and they feared death. But Paul's faith saved them:

> At this rate they knew they would soon be driven ashore; and fearing rocks along the coast, they threw out *four* anchors from the stern and prayed for daylight.
> Some of the sailors planned to abandon the ship, and lowered the emergency boat as though they were going to put out anchors from the prow. But Paul said to the soldiers and commanding officer, "You will all die unless everyone stays aboard." So the soldiers cut the ropes and let the boat fall off.
> As the darkness gave way to the early morning light, Paul begged everyone to eat. "You haven't touched food for

fourteen (1 + 4 = 5) days," he said. "Please eat something now for your own good! For not a hair of your heads shall perish!"

Then he took some hardtack and gave thanks to God before them all, and broke off a piece and ate it. Suddenly everyone felt better and began eating, all *two hundred seventy-six* of us—for that is the number we had aboard.

... So everyone escaped safely ashore. (Acts 27:29-37, 44)

Del Washburn, in his book *Theomatics*, discovered that the unusual number 276 also appears repeatedly as an implicit value multiple associated with Satan's influence and sin. Why would this odd number appear at all in the Bible, explicitly or implicitly? Examine the value closely. The sum of the digits is 2 + 7 + 6 = 15, 1 + 5 = **6**. What do you think the probability is that the implicit value recurring over and over again associated with Satan's influence and sin would sum to the same explicit number symbolic of those topics? As amazing as is that fact alone, there is much more to an examination of this strange but miraculous number. Look at the individual digits. *Two* represents opposites; *seven* represents perfection; and *six* represents Satan's influence and the imperfection of man. Thus, it would seem you have a number that represents the opposite of the perfection intended for man.

Lest this conclusion be questioned, I will draw on one more amazing example of this value. Examine the implicit value of the name *Adam* in Greek:

... Adam ... (Romans 5:14)

Αδαμ

Implicit Value = 1 + 4 + 1 + 40 = 46

Now watch:

46 * **6 = 276**

When you multiply the implicit value for the name of the first man by the number of man, you get the product 276. This is an astonishing result!

So why does the number 276 show up in the story of Paul's shipwreck. Obviously, it specifies the number of people saved from the storm. But beyond the explicit enumeration, it symbolizes the number of souls saved from Satan's power. Since each number of the Bible has both good and bad symbolism around a theme, the number 276 can symbolize both souls saved and souls claimed by Satan, but its inclination is much more toward evil:

... evil. (Genesis 2:9)

ורע

Implicit Value = 6 + 200 + 70 = **276**

... evil. (Matthew 5:39)

τω πονηρω

Implicit Value = 300 + 800 + 80 + 70 + 50 + 8 + 100 + 800 = 2208

2208 = **276** * 8

... die ... (Matthew 26:35)

αποθανειν

Implicit Value = 1 + 80 + 70 + 9 + 1 + 50 + 5 + 10 + 50 = **276**

Here are some examples of the association of the implicit value of 276 with Satan:

How you are fallen from heaven, O Lucifer, son of the morning! (Isaiah 14:12)

איך נפלת משמים הילל בן שחר

Implicit Value = 1 + 10 + 20 + 50 + 80 + 30 + 400 + 40 + 300
+ 40 + 10 + 40 + 5 + 10 + 30 + 30 + 2 + 50 + 300 + 8 + 200
= 1656

1656 = *276* * 6

... "Satan, get behind me! You are looking at this only from a human point of view and not from God's." (Mark 8:33)

υπαγε οπισω μου Σατανα οτι ου φρονεις του Θεου αλλα τα ανθρωπων

Implicit Value = 400 + 80 + 1 + 3 + 5 + 70 + 80 + 10 + 200 +
800 + 40 + 70 + 400 + 200 + 1 + 300 + 1 + 50 + 1 + 70 + 300
+ 10 + 70 + 400 + 500 + 100 + 70 + 50 + 5 + 10 + 200 + 300 +
70 + 400 + 9 + 5 + 70 + 400 + 1 + 30 + 30 + 1 + 300 + 1 + 1 +
50 + 9 + 100 + 800 + 80 + 800 + 50 = 8004

8004 = *276* * 29

"... He gets His power from Beelzebub, the king of demons!" (Luke 11:15)

εν ΒεεζεΒουλ αρχοντι δαιμονιων εκΒαλλει δαιμονια

Implicit Value = 5 + 50 + 2 + 5 + 5 + 7 + 5 + 2 + 70 + 400 +
30 + 1 + 100 + 600 + 70 + 50 + 300 + 10 + 4 + 1 + 10 + 40 +
70 + 50 + 10 + 800 + 50 + 5 + 20 + 2 + 1 + 30 + 30 + 5 + 10 +
4 + 1 + 10 + 40 + 70 + 50 + 10 + 1 = 3036

3036 = *276* * 11

... for he is the father of all liars. (John 8:44)

ψευστης εστιν και ο πατηρ αυτου

Implicit Value = 700 + 5 + 400 + 200 + 300 + 8 + 200 + 5 + 200 + 300 + 10 + 50 + 20 + 1 + 10 + 70 + 80 + 1 + 300 + 9 + 100 + 1 + 400 + 300 + 70 + 400 = 4140

4140 = **276** * 15

And the result of sin without salvation is Hell:

... this place of torment ... (Luke 16:28)

τοπον τουτον βασανου

Implicit Value = 300 + 70 + 80 + 70 + 50 + 300 + 70 + 400 + 300 + 70 + 50 + 2 + 1 + 200 + 1 + 50 + 70 + 400 = 2484

2484 = **276** * 9

... "Away with you, you cursed ones, into the eternal fire prepared for the devil and his demons." (Matthew 25:41)

πορευεσθε απ εμου κατηραμενοι εις το πυρ το αιωνιον το ητοιμασμενον τω διαβολω και τοις αγγελοισ αυτου

Implicit Value = 80 + 70 + 100 + 5 + 400 + 5 + 200 + 9 + 5 + 1 + 80 + 5 + 40 + 70 + 400 + 20 + 1 + 300 + 8 + 100 + 1 + 40 + 5 + 50 + 70 + 10 + 5 + 10 + 200 + 300 + 70 + 80 + 400 + 100 + 300 + 70 + 1 + 10 + 800 + 50 + 10 + 70 + 50 + 300 + 70 + 8 + 300 + 70 + 10 + 40 + 1 + 200 + 40 + 5 + 50 + 70 + 50 + 300 + 800 + 4 + 10 + 1 + 2 + 70 + 30 + 800 + 20 + 1 + 10 + 300 + 70 + 10 + 200 + 1 + 3 + 3 + 5 + 30 + 70 + 10 + 200 + 1 + 400 + 300 + 70 + 400 = 9936

9936 = **276** * 36

But there is an opportunity for rescue from Satan:

So give yourselves humbly to God. Resist the devil and he will flee from you. (James 4:7)

υποταγητε τω Θεω αντιστητε δε τω διαβολω και φευξεται αφ υμων

Implicit Value = 400 + 80 + 70 + 300 + 1 + 3 + 8 + 300 + 5 + 300 + 800 + 9 + 5 + 800 + 1 + 50 + 300 + 10 + 200 + 300 + 8 + 300 + 5 + 4 + 5 + 300 + 800 + 4 + 10 + 1 + 2 + 70 + 30 + 800 + 20 + 1 + 10 + 500 + 5 + 400 + 60 + 5 + 300 + 1 + 10 + 1 + 500 + 400 + 40 + 800 + 50 = 9384

9384 = *276* * 34

And look at the word associated with salvation from the storm in Paul's shipwreck story:

... saved ... (Acts 28:4)

διασωθεντα

Implicit Value = 4 + 10 + 1 + 200 + 800 + 9 + 5 + 50 + 300 + 1 = 1380

1380 = *276* * 5

Summary

With a study of the number *six*, I have completed the last of the *three* physical numbers. It takes the physical nature of the world and the body to the utmost by adding the soul. Like Satan, it holds ambition for perfection but falls through pride and sin, and this failure consumes it. Alternatively, like Jesus, it can represent the ultimate potential of man. Therefore the number *six* is associated with the following:

- Imperfection of man

- Sin

- Satan's influence

- Other angels

- Rule of man

- The man who overcame the physical world and the salvation available to his followers

You have also seen how at the peak of his power, Satan's worldly authorities subjected Jesus to *six* trials that resulted in his execution on the cross. This event could have resulted in a victory for Satan, if Jesus had refused the sentence of death, or if he had remained in the tomb as a victim of death. But Jesus arose from the tomb and thereby conquered Satan and sin.

Seven

Perfection

After the darkness and depravity so prevalent in the number *six*, the number *seven* appears like the bright light of a sunrise on a clear morning. As indicated in earlier chapters, the number *seven* represents perfection. It achieves the perfection that the number *six* cannot. It fulfills the destiny intended for man but forfeited by Adam and Eve in the Garden of Eden. It is the most sacred of numbers. In addition to building on the number *six* by adding the godliness necessary to achieve perfection, the number *seven* can be considered the combination of the spiritual world represented by the number *three* and the physical world represented by the number *four*.

As with the number *three*, the number *seven* often appears in reference to actions by God. The subtle difference between number *three* actions and number *seven* actions is that number *three* actions pertain in some way to the Holy Trinity or God's chosen people; whereas, number *seven* actions pertain to transforming the carnal into the sacred, or similarly, to the fulfillment of divine prophecy. Making holy, setting apart as sacred, consecration, and fulfillment describe the symbolism of the number *seven*.

The *New Scofield Reference Edition* published by Oxford University Press of New York distinguishes *seven dispensations* in the Bible. A *dispensation* is a period of time during which God tests and conditions mankind to make him holy enough to enter the kingdom of heaven. As each dispensation is followed by a new one, the previous conditions continue such that by the end, all *seven* dispensations are in effect. This statement will become clearer when you read the test conditions below. In every dispensation mankind has failed, but salvation is still available to him by God's grace through Jesus Christ. The *seven* dispensations are summarized below:

Dispensation	Test	Result
1. Innocence	Not to sin.	Man disobeyed God and was banished from the Garden of Eden.
2. Moral Responsibility	To do all known good and abstain from all known evil.	Mankind became so evil, God sent the flood to destroy all but one family.
3. Human Government	To protect and serve other people through an established relationship that defines responsibilities of all people to each individual, and constrains each individual's actions.	Mankind failed to rule righteously and governed for self rather than for God.
4. Promise	Blessings to those people who bless Abraham's descendants and curses to those people who persecute the Jews.	Countries, kingdoms, individuals have persecuted the Jews throughout the ages.

5. The Law	Comply with the discipline of the Law in order to take on characteristics of a people who would live in the Kingdom of God.	Israel misinterpreted the Law, sought righteousness through good deeds and ceremonies, violated the Law, and rejected the Messiah.
6. The Church	Spread the Gospel of Jesus Christ's life, death, resurrection, and route to salvation.	Many have rejected the Gospel, and many others have pretended to believe but have become a source of spiritual corruption.
7. The Kingdom	Jesus Christ to rule over the earth for *1000* years.	At the end of the *1000* years, Satan will be released but defeated by Christ and thrown into the lake of fire, at which time the Kingdom will be delivered to God the Father.

Consecration

The term *consecration* means setting apart as sacred. In the Bible, when God declares something as sacred or when he separates his possessions or people from the rest, the number *seven* is usually used. The *seventh* day became the Sabbath, a day of rest and worship. The *seventh* year was considered a Sabbatical year. And the *seventh* occurrence of the *seventh* year was the year of Jubilee.

After six days of creation, God declared the *seventh* day to be sacred:

> So on the *seventh* day, having finished His task, God ceased from this work he had been doing, and God blessed the *seventh* day and declared it holy, because it was the day when He ceased his work of creation. (Genesis 2:2-3)

Noah took more of the sacred animals on the ark than he did the other animals:

> Bring in the animals, too—a *pair* of each, except those kinds I have chosen for eating and for sacrifice: take *seven* pairs of them and *seven* pairs of every kind of bird. (Genesis 7:2-3)

Balaam requested *seven* altars of King Balak so that the king could receive a message from God:

> Balaam said to the king (Balak), "Build *seven* altars here, and prepare *seven* young bulls and *seven* rams for sacrifice." (Numbers 23:1)

When the Israelites entered Egypt to avoid starvation, they remained apart from the Egyptians—a separation that would result in the Israelite exodus years later with greater numbers of people than when they came:

> ... this total of Jacob's household there in Egypt totaled *seventy*. (Genesis 46:27)

> The sons of Jacob and their descendants had lived in Egypt *430* years, and it was on the last day of the *430th* year that all of Jehovah's people left the land. (Exodus 12:40-41)
> (4 + 3 + 0 = 7)

Samson was a Nazirite, dedicated to God, who had never cut his hair:

> She lulled him to sleep with his head in her lap, and they brought in a barber and cut off the *seven* locks of his head ... (Judges 16:19)

Solomon built the Temple in **seven** years:

> ... and the entire building was completed in every detail in November of the *eleventh* year of his reign. So it took *seven* years to build. (1 Kings 6:38)

Enoch did not experience death:

> Enoch, who lived *seven* generations after Adam.... (Jude 1:14)

> Enoch ... when he was *three hundred sixty five*, and in constant touch with God, he disappeared, for God took him! (Genesis 5:21-24)

Actions by God

As discussed above, the number *seven* has a similar symbolism to the number *three* in that the scriptures use both of them in relation to acts of God. At first, they appear to be interchangeable, but there is a subtle difference. The number *three* usually indicates actions by the Trinity, such as Jesus or the Holy Spirit. The number *seven* usually appears when there is a transformation of the carnal into the sacred or similarly where there is fulfillment of divine prophecy.

This distinction does not mean that the number *seven* cannot be associated in any way with Jesus or the Holy Spirit. For example, Jesus utters *seven* cries from the cross:

1. "Father, forgive these people, for they don't know what they are doing." (Luke 23:34)

2. "Today you will be with me in Paradise. This is a solemn promise." (Luke 23:43)
3. When Jesus saw his mother standing by the disciple whom he loved, he said to her, "He is your son." And to the disciple, he said, "She is your mother!" (John 19:25-27)
4. "Eli, Eli, lama sabachthani," which means, "My God, my God, why have you forsaken me?" (Matthew 28:46)
5. "I'm thirsty." (John 19:28)
6. "It is finished." (John 19:30)
7. "Father, I commit my spirit to you." (Luke 23:46)

Even in the above example, Jesus' death and subsequent resurrection represent the fulfillment of ages of divine prophecy and ultimately transformed the dead under the Law into the living under grace. More examples follow.

God instructed Joshua on how to bring down the walls of Jericho:

Your entire army is to walk around the city once a day for six days, followed by *seven* priests walking ahead of the Ark, each carrying a trumpet made from a ram's horn. On the *seventh* day you are to walk around the city *seven* times, with the priests blowing their trumpets. Then, when they give *one* long, loud blast, all the people are to give a mighty shout and the walls of the city will fall down … (Joshua 6:3-5)

Joseph received a promotion for interpreting Pharaoh's dreams:

"Both dreams mean the same thing," Joseph told Pharaoh. "God was telling you what He is going to do here in the land of Egypt. The *seven* fat cows (and also the *seven* fat, well-formed heads of grain) mean that there are *seven* years of prosperity ahead. The *seven* skinny cows (and also the *seven* thin and withered heads of grain) indicate that there will be *seven* years of famine following the *seven* years of prosperity. (Genesis 41:25-27)

Nebuchadnezzar makes a miracle more difficult:

> Then Nebuchadnezzar was filled with fury and his face became dark with anger at Shadrach, Meshach, and Abednego. He commanded that the furnace be heated *seven* times hotter than usual. (Daniel 3:19)

Elisha cures Naaman, the commander of the Syrian army, of leprosy:

> So Naaman arrived with his horses and chariots and stood at the door of Elisha's home. Elisha sent a messenger out to tell him to go and wash in the Jordan River *seven* times and he would be healed of every trace of his leprosy! (2 Kings 5:9-10)

And Jesus had healed Mary Magdalene:

> ... among them were Mary Magdalene (Jesus had cast out *seven* demons from her), Joanna ... (Luke 8:2)

Peter received a guideline for forgiveness:

> Then Peter came to Him and asked "Sir, how often should I forgive a brother who sins against me? *Seven* times?"
> "No!" Jesus replied, *"Seventy* times *seven!"* (Matthew 18:21-22)

Zechariah prophesied of the Messiah, the Branch:

> Listen to me, O Joshua the High Priest, and all you other priests, you are illustrations of the good things to come. Don't you see—Joshua represents my servant the Branch whom I will send. He will be the Foundation Stone of the Temple that Joshua is standing beside, and I will engrave this inscription on it *seven* times: "I will remove the sins of this land in a *single* day." (Zechariah 3:8-9)

The Book of Revelation

In the Book of The Revelation, John has a special affinity for the number *seven*. The number *seven* appears 54 (5 + 4 = 9) times in this book. Because of the number of times it appears in the Book of The Revelation, the number *seven* is the most frequently occurring number in the Bible.

In addition to the explicit uses of the number *seven*, John writes the book of The Revelation around *seven beatitudes* or promises of blessings. John's intent was that the book be read aloud, such that the tone of voice would add another dimension to the message and the structure of the book would be more evident. Here are those *seven* beatitudes:

1. If you read this prophecy aloud to the church, you will receive a special *blessing* from the Lord. Those who listen to it being read and do what it says will also be *blessed*. (The Revelation 1:3)
2. And I heard a voice in the heavens above me saying, "Write this down: At last the time has come for His martyrs to enter into their full reward. Yes, says the Spirit, they are *blest* indeed, for now they shall rest form all their toils and trials; for their good deeds follow them to heaven!" (The Revelation 14:13)
3. Take note: I will come as unexpectedly as a thief! *Blessed* are all who are awaiting Me, who keep their robes in readiness and will not need to walk naked and ashamed. (The Revelation 16:15)
4. ... *Blessed* are those who are invited to the wedding feast of the Lamb. (The Revelation 19:9)
5. *Blessed* and holy are those who share in the First Resurrection. For them the Second Death holds no terrors, for they shall be priests of God and Christ, and shall reign with Him for a *thousand* years. (The Revelation 20:6)
6. Then the angel said to me, "These words are trustworthy and true: 'I am coming soon!' God who tells His prophets what the future holds, has sent His angel to tell you this will

happen soon. *Blessed* are those who believe it and all else written in the scroll." (The Revelation 22:6-7)

7. *Blessed* forever are all who are washing their robes, to have the right to enter in through the gates of the city, and to eat from the tree of Life. (The Revelation 22:14)

John wrote to *seven* churches which established sacred institutions in the land of the Gentiles. The *seven* churches were in the following locations:

1. Ephesus

2. Smyrna

3. Pergamum

4. Thyatira

5. Sardis

6. Philadelphia

7. Laodicea

These churches were real churches at the time John wrote his book, but there were many more churches in existence. It is likely that these churches represent types of churches that will exist throughout the future:

… John to the *seven* churches of Asia … (The Revelation 1:4)

This next reference probably indicates the perfect fullness of the Holy Spirit:

… May you have grace and peace from God who is, and was, and is to come! and from the *seven-fold* Spirit before his throne. (The Revelation 1:4)

The stars and angels in this next scripture symbolize the *seven* churches and their leaders held in honor by Jesus:

> When I turned to see who was speaking, there behind me were *seven* candlesticks of gold. And standing among them was one who looked like Jesus … He held *seven* stars in His right hand …
>
> This is the meaning of the *seven* stars you saw in my right hand, and the *seven* golden candlesticks: The *seven* stars are leaders of the *seven* churches, and the *seven* candlesticks are the churches themselves. (The Revelation 1:12-13, 16, 20)

The book that describes man's fall from grace and salvation through Jesus Christ was sealed with *seven* seals:

> And I saw a scroll in the right hand of the one who was sitting on the throne, a scroll with writing on the inside and on the back, and sealed with *seven* seals. (The Revelation 5:1)

With the breaking of the *seven* seals, comes a series of *seven* judgments symbolized by *seven* trumpets:

> When the Lamb had broken the *seventh* seal, there was silence throughout heaven for what seemed like half an hour. And I saw the *seven* angels that stand before God, and they were given *seven* trumpets. (The Revelation 8:1-2)

Both the Dragon (Satan) and the Beast (Antichrist) are described in similar fashion:

> Suddenly a red Dragon appeared, with *seven* heads and *ten* horns, and *seven* crowns on his heads. (The Revelation 12:3)

> And, now, in my vision, I saw a strange Creature rising up out of the sea. It had *seven* heads and *ten* horns, and *ten* crowns upon its horns. And written on each head were blasphemous

names, each one defying and insulting God. (The Revelation 13:1)

Seven last plagues precede the second coming of Jesus Christ. These plagues represent the wrath of God symbolically contained in *seven* flasks:

> The *seven* angels who were assigned to pour out the *seven* plagues then came from the temple, clothed in spotlessly white linen, with golden belts across their chests. And one of the *four* Living Beings handed each of them a golden flask filled with the terrible wrath of the Living God who lives forever and forever. The temple was filled with smoke from His glory and power; and no one could enter until the *seven* angels had completed pouring out the *seven* plagues. (The Revelation 15:6-8)

Finally, John prophesied of a *seven*-year *tribulation* divided into two, 42 month (each month consisting of 30 days) periods:

> "... They will trample the Holy City for *forty-two* months. And I will give power to my *two* witnesses to prophesy *1260* days clothed in sackcloth." (The Revelation 11:2-3)
>   4 + 2 = *6*
>   1 + 2 + 6 + 0 = *9*

> Then the Dragon encouraged the Creature to speak great blasphemies against the Lord; and gave him authority to control the earth for *forty-two* months. (The Revelation 13:5)

Daniel's Seventy Weeks

As I indicated earlier, one of the great prophets of the Old Testament was Daniel. One aspect of his prophecies is that in some instances he gave specific time periods when his prophecies would come true. In the ninth chapter of the Book of Daniel, the prophet has a vision of 70

(7 + 0 = 7) weeks of years—that is, 70 periods of *seven* years. I will first present the prophecy and then provide an interpretation:

> Even while I was praying and confessing my sin and the sins of my people, and desperately pleading with the Lord my God for Jerusalem, His holy mountain, Gabriel, who I had seen in the earlier vision, flew swiftly to me at the time of the evening sacrifice, and said to me, "Daniel, I am here to help you understand God's plans. The moment you began praying, a command was given, I am here to tell you what it was, for God loves you very much. Listen, and try to understand the meaning of the vision that you saw!
>
> "The Lord has commanded *seventy* weeks of further punishment upon Jerusalem and your people. Then at last they will learn to stay away from sin, and their guilt will be cleansed; then the kingdom of everlasting righteousness will begin, and the Most Holy Place (in the Temple) will be rededicated as the prophets have declared. Now listen! It will be *seven* weeks plus *sixty-two* weeks from the time the command is given to rebuild Jerusalem, until the Anointed One comes! Jerusalem's streets and walls will be rebuilt despite the perilous times.
>
> "After this period of *sixty-two* weeks, the Anointed One will be killed, His kingdom still unrealized … and a king will arise whose armies will destroy the city and the Temple. They will be overwhelmed as with a flood, and war and its miseries are decreed from that time to the very end. This king will make a *seven* year treaty with the people, but after half that time, he will break his pledge and stop the Jews from all their sacrifices; then, as a climax to all his terrible deeds, the Enemy shall utterly defile the sanctuary of God. But in God's time and plan, His judgment will be poured out upon this Evil One." (Daniel 9:20-27)

Daniel prophesied that after 69 (6 + 9 = 15, 1 + 5 = 6) weeks from a decree to rebuild Jerusalem, the Messiah would be killed. Then there would be a time before the last week of *seven* years, which corresponds to the *seven*-year tribulation John writes about in The Revelation. A chronology of relevant events follows:

597 BCE	Babylonians under King Nebuchadnezzar force surrender of King Jehoiachin and destroy Jerusalem
587-586 BCE	King Nebuchadnezzar destroys Solomon's Temple and massively deports Israelites to Babylon
539-538 BCE	The Persians under King Cyrus conquer the Babylonians
539-538 BCE	King Cyrus decrees end to Israelite captivity
520-515 BCE	King Darius decrees that the Israelites can complete rebuilding the Temple—consistent with Jeremiah's prophecy of a *seventy* year exile
457 BCE	King Artaxerxes decrees that Ezra can lead the nation according to the Law of God
445-444 BCE	King Artaxerxes decrees that Nehemiah can rebuild the walls of Jerusalem
7-1 BCE	Birth of Jesus
27-33 CE	Crucifixion of Jesus

Which decree marks the beginning of Daniel's 70 weeks is much debated. Even the number of days in each of Daniel's years is debated. Some theologians argue a normal 365 day solar year, and others argue for a 360 day prophetic year. Earlier in Daniel and in the eleventh chapter of The Revelation, 42 (4 + 2 = 6) months is equated to 1260 (1 +2 + 6 + 0 = 9) days. If the shorter year is used, then the number of years to the Messiah's death is 476 (4 + 7 + 6 = 17, 1 + 7 = 8) rather than 483 (4 + 8 + 3 = 15, 1 + 5 = 6).

There are many formulas proposed to calculate the year, and even the exact day of the Messiah's death. In the following table I use both the solar year and the prophetic year to calculate a range of dates.

Decree	Date of Decree	+483 Years	+476 Years
King Cyrus	539-538 BCE	56-55 BCE	63-62 BCE
King Darius	520-515 BCE	37-32 BCE	44-39 BCE
King Artaxerxes 1st	458-457 BCE	26-27 CE	19-20 BCE
King Artaxerxes 2nd	445-444 BCE	39-40 CE	32-33 BCE

It is not possible to determine the exact date of the decree that marks the beginning of Daniel's 70 weeks. Some theologians argue for a separation by a time of the first *seven* weeks from the following 62 (6 + 2 = 8) weeks. Others argue the prophecy has nothing to do with Jesus. But the prophecies of Daniel were very popular among Jews in the first century BCE and first century CE, and they were very expectant that the Messiah would arrive to free them from Roman domination. As you can see, there are a number of ways the prophecy can point very accurately to the death of Jesus as the Messiah.

The 70th week of *seven* years is separated in the prophecy from the first 69 (6 + 9 = 15, 1 + 5 = 6) weeks. This separation is a real span of time because of the two events prophesied to occur after the end of the 69th week: the killing of the Messiah and the destruction of the Temple. Since Jesus' death occurred in the period of 29-33 CE and the Romans destroyed the Temple in 70 CE, the time between the 69th week and the 70th week is at least 40 years. Of course, the length of this separation had been much longer.

As I indicated above, the 70th week is the same period of *seven* years John calls the tribulation in The Revelation. During this 70th week, the Antichrist will rise to power and be defeated during the war of Armageddon by the second coming of the Messiah. Jesus himself relates this time to his second coming:

"So, when you see the horrible thing (told by Daniel the prophet) standing in a holy place … then those in Judea must flee into the Judean hills. Those on their porches must not even go inside to pack before they flee. Those in the fields should not return to their homes for their clothes.

"And woe to pregnant women and to those with babies in those days. And pray that your flight will not be in winter or on the Sabbath. For their will be persecution such as the world has never before seen in all its history, and will never see again.

"In fact, unless those days are shortened, all mankind will perish. But they will be shortened for the sake of God's chosen people.

"Then if anyone tells you, 'The Messiah has arrived at such and such a place, or has appeared here or there,' don't believe it. For false Christs shall arise, and false prophets, and will do wonderful miracles, so that if it were possible, even God's chosen ones would be deceived. See, I have warned you.

"So if someone tells you the Messiah has returned and is out in the desert, don't bother to go and look. Or, that he is hiding at a certain place, don't believe it! For as the lightning flashes across the sky from east to west, so shall my coming be, when I, the Messiah, return." (Matthew 24:15-27)

The Millennium

After Jesus defeats the Antichrist during the Battle of Armageddon, there will be a period of 1,000 years called the *millennium*. During this period, Jesus Christ will rule on earth, and Satan will be restrained from his evil. There will be universal peace and righteousness:

> Then I saw an angel come down from heaven with the key to the bottomless pit and a heavy chain in his hand. He seized the Dragon—that old serpent, the devil, Satan—and bound him in chains for *1000* years, and threw him into the bottomless pit, which he then shut and locked, so that he could not fool the nations any more until the *thousand* years were finished. (The Revelation 20:1-3)

As you saw in the preceding examination of Daniel's 70 weeks, there is a period of time between the 69th and 70th weeks, followed by the *seven*-year tribulation and then the millennium. Can the numeric code of the Bible predict how long that period of time is? The divine message embedded in the number *seven* is the clue that will help unravel the mystery.

The recorded time in the Bible can logically be divided into periods of thousands of years. References in the scriptures and archaeological evidence indicate that the period of time between Adam and Abraham was approximately 2,000 years. This era can be called the Age of Creation, or the Age of Man. Similar evidence indicates that the period of time between Abraham and Jesus was also approximately 2,000 years. This era can be called the Age of Circumcision, or the Age of The Chosen People. I am using the word *approximately* when referring to the length of these ages because it is impossible to know whether the 2000 year span of these ages is precise or not.

After the second coming of the Messiah, there will be a *millennium*— a period of 1,000 years of Christ's rule on earth and universal peace. What do you have then—two ages of 2,000 years and a prophesied period of 1,000 years—for a total of 5,000 years. How can you determine the period of time between Jesus' death and the second coming of the Messiah?

The other fact at your disposal that provides the answer is that God works in *sevens*:

> For in *six* days the Lord made the heaven, earth, and sea, and everything in them, and rested the *seventh* day; so he blessed the Sabbath day and set it aside for rest. (Exodus 20:11)

But what do the *seven* days of creation have to do with the millennium? If you continue the analogy between the thousands of years and the days of creation, then the millennium of The Revelation is the Sabbath thousand years—a thousand years of peace. That conclusion makes the millennium the *seventh* thousand years. Then you must conclude that the second coming of the Messiah occurs at the end of 6,000 years or 2,000 years from the death of Jesus Christ. One can call this era the Age of Salvation, or the Age of Christianity:

Age	Delineation Points	Length
Age of Man	Adam to Abraham	~2000 years
Age of The Chosen People	Abraham to Jesus	~2000 years
Age of Salvation	Jesus to Second Coming	~2000 years
The Millennium	Second Coming to Release of Satan from Chains	1000 years
Total		**7000** years

This conclusion would indicate that the second coming of the Messiah will occur within the first few decades of the 21st century—and it may be very close. It would explain why the prophecies concerning the end of time have been coming true over the decades of the last century. The Mayan calendar agrees with this prediction. It predicts the end of the current age and beginning of a new era of peace and prosperity (which sounds a lot like the millennium) on December 21, 2012. On the other hand, according to the Jewish calendar, the Jewish year corresponding to the year 2000 is only 5760. This calendar account would indicate there could be over 200 years before the return of the Messiah.

Implicit Values

Because of the in-depth analysis of the number *seven* above, I will give only a few examples of implicit values associated with perfection and the sacred:

The Law of the Old Testament was perfect in the eyes of God:

… the Law (Galatians 4:5)

τον νομον

Implicit Value = 300 + 70 + 50 + 50 + 70 + 40 + 70 + 50 = 700

$$7 + 0 + 0 = 7$$

And keeping with the good-bad spectrum of symbolism, look at this opposite:

... antichrist ... (1 John 4:3)

αυτιχριστου

Implicit Value = 1 + 50 + 300 + 10 + 600 + 100 + 10 + 200 + 300 + 70 + 400 = 2040

$$2 + 0 + 4 + 1 = 7$$

And, when you multiply the foundation number of 111 by *seven*, you get the most precious, perfect acts of God:

... his soul has been made an offering for sin ... (Isaiah 53:10)

אשם נפשו

Implicit Value = 1 + 300 + 40 + 50 + 80 +300 + 6 = **777**

... love of God ... (Romans 8:39)

αγαπης Θεου

Implicit Value = 1 + 3 + 1 + 80 + 8 +200 + 9 + 5 + 70 + 400 = **777**

Summary

Following the *three* physical numbers, the number *seven* adds the grace of God through salvation and thereby achieves perfection. The number *seven* is often used where actions transform the carnal into the sacred. Thus the number *seven* symbolizes the following:

- Perfection

- Making holy

- Setting apart as sacred

- Consecration

- Fulfillment of prophecy

- Opposites of the above, such as the antichrist and fall from grace

I have also explained the key role the number *seven* plays in scripture prophesying the second coming of the Messiah and the end of time. In particular, I have reviewed the special association of the number *seven* with the book of The Revelation and with the prophecies of Daniel. From these prophecies and knowledge of the number *seven*, you can see that both the time of Jesus' death and the time of his second coming have been prophesied. And you can surmise that the time of Jesus' second coming is close.

Eight

Completed Evolution

If the number *seven* represents perfection, then how can you improve beyond it? You might think that logically the numeric code of the Bible would stop after perfection, but, of course, the number *seven* is not the last number in the code. As you have learned, the first *three* numbers of the numeric code are spiritual numbers, and the next *three* numbers in the code are physical numbers. The number *seven* begins a new series of *three* numbers that relate to different aspects of completion. The number *seven* addresses completion as it relates to perfection. The number *eight* approaches completion from a different direction. It symbolizes the evolution from imperfect worldly creations to the next level of existence—as members of the Kingdom of God. Do not be thrown off by the use of the term *evolution*. What is meant here by *evolution* is not the debated theory that in some forms denies the existence of God. I could have substituted the term *development* for *evolution*, but *development* does not connote all the dimensions contained in the term *evolution*. Since the expulsion from the Garden of Eden, mankind has evolved, and the number *eight* is used to describe his progress.

The number *eight* is the perfect symbol of balance or cause and effect. It is associated with having left the carnal world for the spiritual world. Since Old Testament times, the resurrection of the dead has been viewed as a step in man's evolution, so the number *eight* becomes the number symbolizing resurrection. It is associated with faith, as the bridge that allows the unsaved under the Law to be saved through the grace of the Lord. As you will see, the number *eight* also has an association with Jesus as the ultimate man. This association is fitting since Jesus represented man as he needs to be in order to enter the Kingdom of God.

The number *eight* is not one of the more common numbers to appear explicitly in the Bible, but it does occur in some very significant passages. Passages with implicit values revolving around the number *eight* are more common and very revealing. In addition, the number *eight* is very important to the basic message contained in the Bible. As summarized in the *New Scofield Reference Edition*, God's word contains *eight* major *covenants* that explain God's purposes for man. A covenant is a declaration from God that establishes a relationship of responsibility between God and someone(s) else. The *eight* major covenants are:

1. The Covenant of Eden which required Adam to propagate the race, rule the earth and its animals, and abstain from eating from the Tree of Conscience, which gave knowledge of Good and Bad, under penalty of death.
2. The Covenant of Adam which brings hard labor, sorrow, and death to man for his disobedience but also the promise of a redeemer to save man from sin and death.
3. The Covenant of Noah which makes man responsible for the sanctity of life through responsible government, declares that the world will not be destroyed again by flood, and prophecies that the descendants of one of Noah's sons, Shem, will have a special relationship with the Lord.
4. The Covenant of Abraham which establishes the descendants of Abraham as God's chosen people and again promises the Messiah.
5. The Covenant of Moses which defines the Law under which his chosen people would live and therefore be condemned for their failure to live up to the Law.
6. The Covenant of Palestine which prophecies the restoration of the entire promised land to his chosen people following dispersion for disobedience, repentance, and the coming of the Messiah.
7. The Covenant of David which established David's kingdom on earth and promised that the Messiah, who would rule in the future kingdom, would be one of David's descendants.

8. The Covenant of Christ which secures salvation and the forgiveness of sin for the believers in Jesus Christ because he died as a sacrifice for those sins.

These *eight* covenants complete the evolution of mankind from the innocent and then sinful creation in the Garden of Eden to a sacred being worthy of living in the presence of God. Each covenant builds on the covenants before it to guide the evolution, but in the end, man must choose to take advantage of the salvation that is offered. Just as man chose to sin in the beginning, man must choose to return to God.

The Chosen People

The number *eight* appears in scripture when God is selecting people to take mankind to the next level of spiritual evolution. But how is this selection different from the number 12 (1 + 2 = 3) I reviewed in the chapter on the number *three*? There is a subtle difference in emphasis. The number 12 refers to acts of God that result in God selecting his following from the worldly masses and marking them as his own. The evolution associated with the number *eight* works within God's already chosen people. That is, when the number *eight* is used, there is an implied assumption that the action associated with 12 has already occurred. The number *eight* emphasizes the point of evolution rather than the act of selection. It symbolizes the death of the old life and the beginning of a new life—a higher order of existence.

The rite of circumcision took the Israelis from being loyal followers of God to being God's chosen people:

> Every male shall be circumcised on the *eighth* day after birth. This applies to every foreign-born slave as well as to everyone born in your household. This is a permanent part of this contract, and it applies to all your posterity. All must be circumcised. Your bodies will thus be marked as participants in my everlasting covenant. Anyone who refuses these terms

shall be cut off from his people, for he has violated my contract. (Genesis 17:12-14)

Only *eight* people were saved from the flood that destroyed the corrupt world. They became the progenitors of the new world:

But Noah had gone into the boat that very day with his wife and his sons, Shem, Ham, and Japheth, and their wives. (Genesis 7:13)

Yet only *eight* people were saved from drowning in that terrible flood. (1 Peter 3:20)

Having transitioned from the physical world to the spiritual world, Moses reached an age when he was prepared to see Pharaoh:

Moses was *eighty* years old and Aaron *eighty-three* at this time of their confrontation with Pharaoh. (Exodus 7:7)

Chosen by God and anointed by Samuel, David established a royal lineage that was to include the Messiah. He was the *eighth* son of Jesse:

David was the son of aging Jesse who was a member of the tribe of Judah and lived in Bethlehem-Judah and had *eight* sons. (1 Samuel 17:11)

Joseph was 17 (1 + 7 = 8) when he entered Egypt:

Jacob's son Joseph was now *seventeen* years old ... So when the Midianites came by, his brothers pulled Joseph out of the well and sold him to them for *twenty* pieces of silver, and they took him along to Egypt. (Genesis 37:2, 28)

And after Jacob joined his son in Egypt, he lived the same number of years there:

> So Israel lived in the land of Goshen in Egypt—and soon the people of Israel began to prosper, and there was a veritable population explosion among them. Jacob lived *seventeen* years after his arrival. (Genesis 47:27-28)
>   1 + 7 = *8*

The number *eight* is significant in the description of the inner court of the future Temple as prophesied by Ezekiel:

> The only difference was that it had *eight* steps leading up to it instead of *seven*. (Ezekiel 40:31)

> So, in all, there were *eight* tables, four inside and four outside, where the sacrifices were cut up and prepared. (Ezekiel 40:41)

Resurrection

The Bible speaks of *two* resurrections at the end of time. One resurrection is for the righteous to eternal life in the presence of God. Another resurrection is for the unrighteous to damnation and banishment from God's presence. Both constitute evolution to the next level of existence or the next order of being. Consequently, there are *eight* resurrections of individuals by another person recorded in the Bible.

| 1. The widow's son by Elijah | 1 Kings 17:17-24 | But one day the woman's son became sick and died … And the Lord heard Elijah's prayer, and the sprit of the child returned, and he became alive again! |

2. The son of a woman from Shunem by Elisha	2 Kings 4:18-37	When Elisha arrived, the child was indeed dead, lying there upon the prophet's bed. He went in and shut the door behind him and prayed to the Lord … And the child's body began to grow warm again!
3. A man whose body was thrown in Elisha's tomb	2 Kings 13:20-21	So Elisha died and was buried. In those days bandit gangs of Moabites used to invade the lands each spring. Once some men who were burying a friend spied these marauders so they hastily threw his body into the tomb of Elisha. And as soon as the body touched Elisha's bones, the dead man revived and jumped to his feet!
4. The rabbi's daughter by Jesus	Matthew 9:23-26	When Jesus arrived at the rabbi's home and saw the noisy crowds and heard the funeral music, he said, "Get them out, for the littler girl isn't dead; she is only sleeping!" … Jesus went in where the little girl was lying and took her by the hand, and she jumped up and was all right again!

5. The widow's son by Jesus	Luke 7:11-17	A funeral procession was coming out as Jesus approached the village gate. The boy who had died was the only son of his widowed mother ... Then he walked over to the coffin and touched it, and the bearers stopped. "Laddie," he said, "come back to life again." Then the boy sat up and began to talk to those around him!
6. Lazarus by Jesus	John 11:17-44	Then they came to the tomb. It was a cave with a heavy stone rolled across its door ... for he has been dead *four* days ... So they rolled the stone aside ... Then Jesus shouted, "Lazarus, come out!" And Lazarus came—bound up in the grave cloth, his face muffled in a head swath. Jesus told them, "Unwrap him and let him go!"
7. Tabitha by Peter	Acts 9:36-42	... as soon as Peter arrived, they took him upstairs where Tabitha lay ... Turning to the body he said, "Get up, Tabitha," and she opened her eyes! And when she saw Peter, she sat up!

8. Eutychus by Paul	Acts 20:7-10	... and as Paul spoke on and on, a young man named Eutychus, sitting on the window sill, went fast asleep, and fell *three* stories to his death below. Paul went down and took him into his arms. "Don't worry", he said, "he's all right!" And he was!

You will notice Jesus' resurrection is not included in the above list. The above people were raised to life but would experience a natural death again. Jesus conquered death and ascended to heaven. His resurrection is the only one to date that previews the resurrection from physical form to spirit in the presence of God that is yet to come.

Association with Jesus as the Ultimate Man

As you will see in more detail with the implicit values, the number *eight* has a special association with Jesus, who represents the completion of the development of man. Jesus is the ultimate man—not just free of sin, but complete in every way and in harmony with the Father. Following his death and resurrection, Jesus received the first resurrected, eternal body capable of living within the presence of God.

The number *eight* appears in connection with the transfiguration of Christ, when Jesus revealed his heavenly glory to his disciples:

Eight days later He took Peter, James, and John with Him into the hills to pray. And as He was praying, His face began to shine, and His clothes became dazzling white and blazed with light. (Luke 9:28)

Eight days passed before the belief of all of the disciples was complete:

> *Eight* days later the disciples were together again, and this time Thomas was with them. The doors were locked; but suddenly, as before, Jesus was standing among them and greeting them. (John 20:26)

Implicit Values

When you look at the above explicit examples of the use of the number *eight*, you should be able to discern a common thread running through them: faith. When Abraham adopted the rite of circumcision, he was expressing his faith in God and his promises. Noah endured continuous ridicule as he built the ark, because he believed God when he said he would send rain. Moses' faith allowed him to confront Pharaoh and deliver his people. And David's faith brought him victory over Goliath and eventually the kingdom of Israel. Finally, who can question the faith it takes to raise the dead or the faith of Jesus or his disciples?

It is through faith that people find the strength necessary to take those giant steps into the unknown that are vital for evolution. And it is with faith that God sent his Son Jesus as a lasting sacrifice for man's sins that completes man's evolution and allows man to live in the presence of God.

Look at the implicit value of the word *faith* and also one of the more famous actions associated with faith:

> … faith … (Matthew 9:22)

> πιστις

> Implicit Value = 80 + 10 + 200 + 300 + 10 + 200 = 800

> 8 + 0 + 0 = *8*

… follow me … (Mark 8:34)

ακολουθειτω μοι

Implicit Value = 1 + 20 + 70 + 30 + 70 + 400 + 9 + 5 + 10 +
300 + 800 + 40 + 70 + 10 = 1835

1 + 8 + 3 + 5 = 17

1 + 7 = 8

Both heaven and earth were created perfectly in their ultimate form:

… heaven … (Genesis 1:1)

תשמים

Implicit Value = 5 + 300 + 40 + 10 + 40 = 395

3 + 9 + 5 = 17

1 = 7 = 8

… earth … (Genesis 1:1)

הארץ

Implicit Value = 5 + 1 + 200 + 90 = 296

2 + 9 + 6 = 17

1 + 7 = 8

Amazingly, the name of God, Jehovah, or more accurately, Yahweh,
has the same implicit value:

Jehovah, or Yahweh

יהוה

Implicit Value = 10 + 5 + 6 + 5 = 26

2 + 6 = *8*

As does the Holy Spirit:

… Spirit … (John 14:26)

πνευμα αγιον

Implicit Value = 80 + 50 + 5 + 400 + 40 + 1 + 1 + 3 + 10 + 70 + 50 = 710

7 + 1 = *8*

There is also the association of the number *eight* with Jesus, especially with his resurrection. The implicit values of the following scriptures associate Jesus with the completely evolved man. As the Messiah, he is man as God intended man to be. When he conquered death, he was the first man to receive a resurrected body:

Yeshua
Name of Jesus in Hebrew

ישוע

Implicit Value = 10 + 300 + 6 + 70 = 386

3 + 8 + 6 = 17

1 + 7 = *8*

... Son of Man ... (Mathew 16:27)

υιος του ανθρωπου

Implicit Value = 400 + 10 + 70 + 200 + 300 + 70 + 400 + 1 + 50 + 9 + 100 + 800 + 80 + 70 + 400 = 2960

2 + 9 + 6 + 0 = 17

1 + 7 = *8*

... the Messiah (John 1:41)

του Μεσσιαν

Implicit Value = 300 + 70 + 50 + 40 + 5 + 200 + 200 + 10 + 1 + 50 = 926

9 + 2 + 6 = 17

1 + 7 = *8*

... Christ, the savior ... (John 1:41)

σωτηρ Χριστος

Implicit Value = 200 + 800 + 300 + 8 + 100 + 600 + 100 + 10 + 200 + 300 + 70 + 200 = 2888

2 + 8 + 8 + 8 = 24

2 + 6 = *8*

... day he will be raised to life again ... (Matthew 20:19)

ημερα εγερθησεται

Implicit Value = 8 + 40 + 5 + 100 + 1 + 5 + 3 + 5 + 100 + 9 + 8 + 200 + 5 + 300 + 1 + 10 = 800

$$8 + 0 + 0 = 8$$

I have covered repeatedly how the symbolism of numbers has both positive and negative symbolism around a common theme. I promised earlier an interesting fact associated with the Hebrew form of the name Satan. You have seen above the implicit values of the Holy Trinity. Now look at the implicit value of the name Satan in Hebrew:

... Satan ... (1 Chronicles 21:1)

שטן

Implicit Value = 300 + 9 + 50 = 359

$$3 + 5 + 9 = 17$$

$$1 + 7 = 8$$

But the interesting fact is not that you end up with the implicit value of *eight*. The amazing fact that once again proves the divine hand in the writing of scripture is that the first use of the name Satan appears in 1 Chronicles 21:1. The twenty-first chapter of 1 Chronicles is the 359th chapter of the Bible. That is right. The name Satan, which has an implicit value of 359, first appears in the 359th chapter of the Bible.

The Name of Jesus

The most amazing use of the number *eight* in an implicit value is the value of the name *Jesus*. I added up the numeric values of the Greek letters in the name Jesus in the first chapter. Perhaps you remember the total. It was 888. Now look at the name Jesus in Greek again—*Ιησους*:

Name of Jesus in Greek

$$I = 10$$

$$\eta = 8$$

$$\sigma = 200$$

$$o = 70$$

$$\upsilon = 400$$

$$\varsigma = 200$$

Total Value = 888

$$8 + 8 + 8 = 24$$

$$2 + 4 = \mathbf{6}$$

Examine the value of 888. In the chapter on the number *one*, I introduced the use in scripture of the implicit value 37. Once again, the number 37 is a prime number, that is, only divisible by itself and one. It has a special association with Jesus in scripture explained by the individual digits (*three* and *seven*) and the sum of its digits which equates to *one*. It represents the act of God sending his perfect son, Jesus, to earth to die as a sacrifice to wash away man's sins. You also learned that when you multiply 37 times *three*—an act of God—you get the number 111, and this number also has a special association with Jesus and the Holy Spirit as members of the divine Trinity.

Now, multiply the number 111 by *eight* to complete the evolution. You get the product 888. That the number 888 should also represent the numeric value of Jesus' name is one of the great miracles of the numbers of the Bible. That you could start with the number 37, multiply it by the number *three*—which has a special association with Jesus—then multiply that product by *eight*—which completes the evolution of man to a higher order—and get the numeric value of Jesus' name is one of the divine threads that interweaves the fabric of God's word. Finally, if you reduce the value of name of Jesus (8 + 8 + 8 = 24, 2 + 4 =*6*), you get the number *six*. Jesus is the ultimate man. Once again, you have a demonstration that God is the one and only author of the Bible.

Here are two Old Testament examples of the implicit value 888 that tie well with their New Testament counterparts:

For I am the Lord—I do not change. (Malachi 3:6)

אני יהוה לא שניתי

Implicit Value = 1 + 50 + 10 + 10 + 5 + 6 + 5 + 30 + 1 + 300 + 50 + 10 + 400 + 10 = *888*

... salvation of our God. (Isaiah 52:10)

ישועת אלהינו

Implicit Value = 10 + 300 + 6 + 70 + 400 + 1 + 30 + 5 + 10 + 50 + 6 = *888*

... The Lord our God is the *one* and only God. (Mark 12:29)

κυριος Θεος κυριος εις εστιν

Implicit Value = 20 + 400 + 100 + 10 + 70 + 200 + 9 + 5 + 70 + 200 + 20 + 400 + 100 + 10 + 70 + 200 + 5 + 10 + 200 + 5 + 200 + 300 + 10 + 50 = 2664

2664 = *888* * 3

... Rabbi, you are the Son of God. (John 1:49)

ραββι συ ει υιοσ του Θεου

Implicit Value = 100 + 1 + 2 + 2 + 10 + 200 + 400 + 5 + 10 + 400 + 10 + 70 + 200 + 300 + 70 + 400 + 9 + 5 + 70 + 400 = 2664

2664 = *888* * 3

As a final example, you have the verse that describes the earlier Christians meeting on Sunday rather than on Saturday, the traditional Sabbath. Christianity represented the new order:

On the first day of the week, we gathered for a communion service ... (Acts 20:7)

εν δε τη μια των σαββατων συνηγμενων ημων κλασαι αρτον

Implicit Value = 5 + 50 + 4 + 5 + 300 + 8 + 40 + 10 + 1 + 300 + 800 + 50 + 200 + 1 + 2 + 2 + 1 + 300 + 800 + 50 + 200 + 400 + 50 + 8 + 3 + 40 + 5 + 50 + 800 + 50 + 8 + 40 + 800 + 50 + 20 + 30 + 1 + 200 + 1 + 10 + 1 + 100 + 300 + 70 + 50 = 6216

6216 = *888* * 7

Summary

The number *eight* is the second of *three* numbers that symbolize different aspects of completion. The number *eight* represents the completion of man's evolution from sinful creations driven from the Garden of Eden to spiritually complete beings worthy of living in the presence of God. I summarize the number *eight* below:

- Completed evolution

- Faith

- Fulfillment of intent

- Chosen people

- Resurrection

- Jesus as the ultimate man

In this examination of the number *eight*, I have also completed an implicit value chain that began with the number 37, became the interim value of 111, and ended with 888—the implicit value of the name Jesus in Greek. This numeric thread that runs through the tapestry of the Bible simultaneously points to Jesus as the type of person all should strive to become, and while it reveals God as the one and only author of the Bible.

Nine

The Ending

With the number *nine*, the journey through the divine numeric code of the Bible ends. Like the number *eight*, the number *nine* does not appear explicitly in its simplest form very often. But both the explicit use of the number *nine*, and other well-known numbers which sum to the number *nine*, are very significant to the message of the Bible. The number *nine* is the third of the *three* numbers symbolizing different aspects of completion. Since the number *nine* is also the last of the numbers in the biblical code, its meaning is as logical as you should expect. The number *nine* is the symbol of what brings things to an end.

There are examples of this symbolism in everyday life. For example, the *ninth* month ends a woman's pregnancy and results in a new life. The ninth planet ends the reach of the known solar system. And of course, within the Arabic numeral system, the number *nine* is the last digit before you add another position and begin again.

As with the numbers before it, the number *nine* builds on the immediately previous number by adding another dimension. The number *eight* symbolizes completion—but not in the sense of an ending. While the number *eight* symbolizes completion in the sense of completed development, or making entire, or fulfillment of intent, the number *nine* adds the meaning of finality. It represents the end or conclusion.

When it appears explicitly in the scripture, it carries with it this connotation of conclusion—the end of a life or the end of a state of being. When other well-known numbers with combinations of digits that add to the number *nine* appear explicitly in the Bible, they often have even a more specific symbolism: the end of time.

End of a State of Being

The end of a state of being can pertain to many things, even the end of life, though I will examine that ending separately. The following scriptures include the number *nine*, or combinations of digits that add to *nine*, in a variety of contexts but with always the same symbolism of an ending.

Abraham ended the obscurity of his people, setting them aside as the chosen race, at the age of 99 (9 + 9 = 18, 1 + 8 = **9**):

> Abraham was *ninety-nine* years old at the time, and Ishmael was thirteen. Both were circumcised the same day, along with all the other men and boys of the household, whether born there or bought as slaves. (Genesis 17:24-27)

Sarah's barrenness ended at 90 (9 + 0 = **9**):

> Then Abraham threw himself down in worship before the Lord, but inside he was laughing in disbelief! "Me, be a father?" he said in amusement. "Me—*100* years old? And Sarah, to have a baby at *90*?" (Genesis 17:17)

The end of servitude to the Moabites came with Ehud:

> For the next *eighteen* years the people of Israel were required to pay crushing taxes to King Eglon.
> But when they cried to the Lord, he sent them a savior, Ehud (son of Gera, a Benjamite) ...
> ... So Moab was conquered by Israel that day. (Judges 3:14-15, 30)
> 1 + 8 = **9**

The *ninth* year of their rulers' reign played a key role in the end of freedom for both the kingdom of Israel and the kingdom of Judah:

> Now the land of Israel was filled with Assyrian troops for *three* years besieging Samaria, the capital city of Israel. Finally,

in the *ninth* year of King Hoshea's reign, Samaria fell and the people of Israel were exiled to Assyria. (2 Kings 17:5-6)

Then King Nebuchadnezzar of Babylon mobilized his entire army and laid siege to Jerusalem, arriving on March 25 of the *ninth* year of the reign of King Zedekiah of Judah. (2 Kings 25:17)

The end of Jewish persecution in Babylon revolved around a statue and the defiance of *three* Jewish youths:

King Nebuchadnezzar made a golden statue *ninety* feet high and *nine* feet wide and set it up on the Plain of Dura, in the province of Babylon … this is the king's command:

"When the band strikes up, you are to fall flat on the ground and worship King Nebuchadnezzar's golden statue; anyone who refuses to obey will immediately be thrown into a flaming furnace."

… But some officials went to the king and accused some of the Jews of refusing to worship!

"Your Majesty," they said to him, "… there are some Jews out there—Shadrach, Meshach, and Abednego, who you have put in charge of Babylonian affairs—who have defied you …"

… Then Nebuchadnezzar was filled with fury and his face became dark with anger at Shadrach, Meshach, and Abednego. He commanded the furnace be heated up *seven* times hotter than usual, and called for some of the strongest men of his army to bind Shadrach, Meshach, and Abednego, and throw them into the fire.

So they bound them tight with ropes and threw them into the furnace, fully clothed. And because the king, in his anger, had demanded such a hot fire in the furnace, the flames leaped out and killed the soldiers as they threw them in! …

But suddenly as he was watching, Nebuchadnezzar jumped up in amazement and exclaimed to his advisors, "Didn't we throw *three* men into the furnace?"

"Yes," they said, "we did indeed, Your Majesty."

"Well, look!" Nebuchadnezzar shouted. "I see *four* men, unbound, walking around in the fire, and they aren't even hurt by the flames! And the *fourth* looks like a god!"

... "Shadrach, Meshach, and Abednego, servants of the Most High God! Come out! Come here!" So they stepped out of the fire.

... Then Nebuchadnezzar said, "Blessed be the God of Shadrach, Meshach, and Abednego, for he sent an angel to deliver his trusting servants when they defied the king's commandment, and were willing to die rather than serve or worship any god except their own. Therefore, I make this decree, that any person of any nation, language, or religion who speaks a word against the God of Shadrach, Meshach, and Abednego shall be torn limb from limb and his house knocked into a heap of rubble. (Daniel 3:1-29)

Jesus ended a woman's suffering after 18 (1 + 8 = **9**) years:

One Sabbath as he was teaching in a synagogue, he saw a seriously handicapped woman who had been bent double for *eighteen* years and was unable to straighten herself.

Calling her over to him, Jesus said, "Woman, you are healed of your sickness!" He touched her, and instantly she could stand straight. (Luke 13:10-13)

End of Life

The number *nine* appears prominently in the account of the ending of the most significant life ever: the life of Jesus. Note the combinations of numbers in the passage below: the *three* hours during which Jesus was dying, the *sixth* hour during which sin seemed triumphant, and the *ninth* hour brought the death of Jesus. It is not mentioned that on the *third* day Jesus arose, conquering both sin and death:

That afternoon the whole earth was covered with darkness for *three* hours, from the *sixth* to the *ninth* hour. (Matthew 27:45)

The End of Time

The number *nine* has special symbolism relating to the end of time. Whether it be the Jews watching for the coming of the Messiah or the Christians waiting for the second coming of Christ, the end of time is a theme that runs through both the Old and New Testaments. You may be surprised how often the number *nine* appears in relation to these prophecies. I will review some of these examples later in this chapter.

A not-so-obvious use of the number *nine* in reference to the end of time occurs at the beginning of the Sermon on the Mount. This sermon is among the most famous in the Bible. It contains what are called the *beatitudes*, or promises of blessings at the end of time. Count as you read them below:

One day as the crowds were gathering, He went up the hillside with His disciples and sat down and taught them there.

"Blessed are humble men, for the Kingdom of Heaven is given to them.

"Blessed are those who mourn, for they shall be comforted.

"Blessed are the meek and lowly, for the whole wide world belongs to them.

"Blessed are those who long to be just and good, for they shall be completely satisfied.

"Blessed are the kind and merciful, for they shall be shown mercy.

"Blessed are those whose hearts are pure, for they shall see God.

"Blessed are those who strive for peace—they shall be called the sons of God.

"Blessed are those who are persecuted because they are good, for the Kingdom of Heaven is theirs.

"Blessed are you when you are reviled and persecuted and lied about because you are my followers—wonderful! Be happy about it! Be very glad!

For a tremendous reward awaits you up in heaven." (Matthew 5:1-12)

What was Jesus trying to say with the beatitudes? These *nine* beatitudes describe the characteristics of a follower of Christ. In like manner, they describe a subject within the Kingdom of God. In return for taking on these characteristics, the believer is promised a place in the Kingdom of God at the end of the current age.

Implicit Values

Before I continue with the number *nine*, look at some examples of scriptures with the implicit value of *nine*. There are more examples to follow with a slightly different symbolism. Here, I include a few examples for completeness so you will know that all of these divine numbers, whether explicitly or implicitly used, have the meanings presented in this book—specifically that in this book the number *nine* carries with it the symbolism of an ending.

The Revelation is the final book of the Bible. In its original Greek form, it begins with the word *apocalypse*, usually translated as *the revelation*, and ends with the word *amen*. Now watch:

The revelation … (The Revelation 1:1)

Αποκαλυψις

Implicit Value = 1 + 80 + 70 + 20 + 1 + 30 + 400 + 700 + 10 + 200 = 1512

$$1 + 5 + 1 + 2 = 9$$

… amen (The Revelation 22:11)

αμην

Implicit Value = 1 + 40 + 8 + 50 == 99

$$9 + 9 = 18$$

$$1 + 8 = 9$$

In The Revelation the name Alpha and Omega is used *nine* times to refer to the All Powerful God:

... Alpha and Omega ... (The Revelation 1:8)

α ω

Implicit Value = 1 + 800 = 801

$$8 + 0 + 1 = 9$$

Following are other words and phrases with the implicit value of *nine*:

The one sitting on the throne ... (The Revelation 7:15)

και καθημενος επι του θρονου

Implicit Value = 20 + 1 + 10 + 20 + 1 + 9 + 8 + 40 + 5 + 50 + 70 + 200 + 5 + 80 + 10 + 300 + 70 + 400 + 9 + 100 + 70 + 50 + 70 + 400 = 1998

$$1 + 9 + 9 + 8 = 27$$

$$2 + 7 = 9$$

... the Truth ... (John 14:6)

εγω ειμι η οδος και η αληθεια και η ζωη

Implicit Value = 8 + 1 + 30 + 8 + 9 + 5 + 10 + 1 = 72

$$7 + 2 = 9$$

... the narrow gate (Matthew 7:13)

της στενης πυλης

Implicit Value = 300 + 8 + 200 + 200 + 300 + 5 + 50 + 8 + 200 + 80 + 400 + 30 + 8 + 200 = 1989

$1 + 9 + 8 + 9 = 27$

$2 + 7 + 9$

... the door ... (Luke 13:25)

την θυραν

Implicit Value = 300 + 8 + 50 + 9 + 400 + 100 + 1 + 50 = 918

$9 + 1 + 8 = 18$

$1 + 8 = 9$

And lest you forget the darker side of the number, I must include the negative symbolism as well:

... name of the beast ... (The Revelation 13:17)

ονομα θηριου

Implicit Value = 70 + 50 + 70 + 40 + 1 + 9 + 8 + 100 + 10 + 70 + 400 = 828

$8 + 2 + 8 = 18$

$1 + 8 = 9$

The Number and Implicit Value—144

Do you remember reading the number 144 (1 + 4 + 4 = 9) in the Bible? The number 144 is a significant number in the Bible in its own right. It occurs multiple times both explicitly and implicitly. Most often, when it is discussed by Bible analysts, it is included in the same contexts as the number 12 (1 + 2 = 3) as if there were no difference in meaning—just an amplification of the same meaning. This mistake is very common and not without reason.

As you learned earlier, the number 12 is a special variant of the number *three*, that represents the special act of God whereby he chooses his following from the worldly masses. The number 144 is not only a multiple of the number 12; it is its square, that is, 144 = 12 * 12. And the number 144 carries a symbolism similar to the number 12 in that it represents the chosen.

But look at the number 144 more closely by adding its digits as you have become accustomed to doing: 1 + 4 + 4 = **9**. Now, you can see that the number 144 is not just an amplification of the number 12 but carries with it another variant to the symbolism, that is, the chosen at the end of time. Look at a few explicit uses of the number:

At the end of time, 144,000 (1 + 4 + 4 + 0 + 0 + 0 = 9) will receive the Seal of God:

> … hurt neither the earth nor sea or trees—until we have placed the Seal of God upon the foreheads of His servants.
> How many were given this mark? I heard the number—it was **144,000**. (The Revelation 7:3-4)

> Then I saw a Lamb standing on Mount Zion in Jerusalem, and with Him were **144,000** who had His Name and His Father's Name written on their foreheads. And I heard a sound from heaven like the roaring of a great waterfall or the rolling of mighty thunder. It was the singing of a choir accompanied by harps.

This tremendous choir—*144,000* strong—sang a wonderful new song in front of the throne of God ... (The Revelation 14:1-3)

The new Jerusalem will have walls *144* (1 + 4 + 4 = *9*) cubits wide:

Then he measured the thickness of the walls and found them to be *144* cubits by human measurements. (The Revelation 21:17)

If these explicit uses of the number 144 are not enough to convince you of the divine symbolism embedded in the number, the implicit uses are equally amazing. First look at the word *elect*, which means *the ones God has chosen*:

... the elect ... (Romans 11:7)

η εκλογη

Implicit Value = 8 + 5 + 20 + 30 + 70 + 3 + 8 = *144*

As I have done previously, I will quote the implicit values of the following scriptures using the concept of multiples and, in this case, multiples of the number 144. But if you follow through with the math and add the digits of any product of the multiple, you will result in the number *nine*. An example will make this statement more clear. Take the number *144* and multiply it by any other number, say 32. The result is a number for which the sum of its digits equals *nine*:

144 * 32 = 4608

4 + 6 + 0 + 8 = 18

1 + 8 = *9*

You can try this experiment combining the number 144 with any other number, and you will always get this result. This amazing fact is just another piece of evidence that points to the use of this number with the symbolism of the end of time. More examples of implicit values involving 144 follow.

Lazarus was selected for perhaps Jesus' greatest miracle and symbolizes the resurrection to come:

... Lazarus ... (John 11:43)

Λαζαρε

Implicit Value = 30 + 1 + 7 + 1 + 100 + 5 = **144**

... the ones coming out of the Great Tribulation ... (The Revelation 7:14)

ερχομενοι εκ της θλιψεως της μεγαλης

Implicit Value = 5 + 100 + 600 + 70 + 40 + 5 + 50 + 70 + 10 + 5 + 20 + 300 + 8 + 200 + 9 + 30 + 10 + 700 + 5 + 800 + 200 + 300 + 8 + 200 + 40 + 5 + 3 + 1 + 30 + 8 + 200 = 4032

4032 = **144** * 28

... saints ... (The Revelation 8:3)

αγιων

Implicit Value = 1 + 3 + 10 + 800 + 50 = 864

864 = **144** * 6

... those whose names are written in the Lamb's Book of Life. (The Revelation 21:27)

γεγραμμενοι εν τω βιβλιω ζωης του αρνιου

Implicit Value = 3 + 5 + 3 + 100 + 1 + 40 + 40 + 5 + 50 + 70
+ 10 + 5 + 50 + 300 + 800 + 2 + 10 + 2 + 30 + 10 + 800 + 7
+ 800 + 8 + 200 + 300 + 70 + 400 + 1 + 100 + 50 + 10 + 70 +
400 = 4752

4752 = *144* * 33

The Number and Implicit Value—666

Previously, in the chapter on the number *six*, I quoted the scripture from the book of The Revelation that contains perhaps the most notorious number in the Bible. Look at it again:

> He required everyone—great and small, rich and poor, slave and free—to be tattooed with a certain mark on the right hand or on the forehead. And no one could get a job or even buy in any store without the permit of that mark, which was either the name of the Creature or the code number of his name. Here is a puzzle that calls for careful thought to solve it. Let those who are able, interpret this code: the numeric values of the letters in his name add to *666*! (The Revelation 13:16-18)
> 6 + 6 + 6 = 18
> 1 +8 = *9*

Because of the notoriety of this number and its attachment to the Antichrist at the end of time, you might believe that this scripture is the only explicit use of the number 666 in the Bible. But that assumption would be mistaken. The number appears another time in the Old Testament. Look in the tenth chapter of 1 Kings. The amount of King Solomon's annual tribute from the known carnal world at the height of the Empire of Israel was 666 talents of gold:

> Each year Solomon received *666* talents of gold, besides sales taxes and profit from trade with the kings of Arabia and the other surrounding territories. (1 Kings 10:14-15)

What is the likelihood that these two uses of the same number have no relation to one another? What are the chances that this second occurrence of the number 666 is coincidence? Given everything you have learned in the previous chapters, you should realize by now that there is no possibility these two occurrences are mere coincidence.

Look at what happens to King Solomon immediately after the first reference. The first set of scriptures that follows is a continuation of the description of King Solomon's empire at its height, or as it turns out, its end. The second set of scriptures comes immediately after:

So King Solomon was richer and wiser than all the kings of the earth. Great men from many lands came to interview him and listen to his God-given wisdom. They brought him annual tribute of silver and gold dishes, beautiful cloth, myrrh, spices, horses, and mules.

Solomon built up a great stable of horses with a vast number of chariots, and cavalry—*1,400* chariots in all, and *12,000* cavalrymen who lived in the chariot cities and with the king at Jerusalem. Silver was as common as stones in Jerusalem in those days, and cedar was of no greater value than the common sycamore! (1 Kings 10:23-27)

Now watch what happens in the immediately following verses:

King Solomon married many other girls besides the Egyptian princess. Many of them came from nations where idols were worshipped—Moab, Ammon, Edom, Sidon, and from the Hittites—even though the Lord had clearly instructed His people not to marry into those nations, because the women they married would get them started worshipping their gods. Yet Solomon did it anyway. He had *seven hundred* wives and *three hundred* concubines; and sure enough, they turned his heart away from the Lord, especially in his old age. They encouraged him to worship their gods instead of trusting completely in the Lord as his father David had done. Solomon worshipped Ashtoreth, the goddess of the Sidonians, and Milcom, the horrible god of the Ammonites. Thus Solomon did what was clearly wrong and refused to follow the Lord as his father David had done. He even built a temple on the Mount of Olives, across the valley from Jerusalem, for Chemosh, the depraved god of Moab, and another for Molech, the unutterably vile god of the Ammonites. Solomon built temples for these foreign wives to use for burning incense and sacrificing to their gods.

Jehovah was very angry with Solomon about this, for now Solomon was no longer interested in the Lord God of Israel who had appeared to him twice to warn him specifically against worshipping other gods. But he hadn't listened, so now the Lord said to him, "Since you have not kept our agreement and have not obeyed my laws, I will tear the kingdom away from you and your family and give it to someone else. (1 Kings 11:1-11)

So you see from the above sets of scriptures that at the height of King Solomon's empire, when wealth and materialism was at its peak, King Solomon turned away from God, and thus ended his royal line.

Now what does that historical account have to do with the occurrence of the number 666 in the book of The Revelation? Look at the number 666. It is composed of *three sixes* that total to 18 which equates to *nine* (1 + 8 = 9). In the chapter on the number *three*, I examined a similar number (the number 111) which symbolizes the Holy Trinity. I know it represents the Holy Trinity for three primary reasons: 1) its root prime number is 37, which equates to the number *one* (3 + 7 = 10, 1 + 0 = *1*), the number associated with God; 2) if you multiply the number 37 by the number *three* (an act of God), then you get 111; and 3) the number 111 is composed of *three ones*, symbolizing *three* divine entities or the Holy Trinity.

Can you see the similarity between the number 111 and the number 666? If you multiply the number 111 by *six*, the number symbolizing worldly imperfection, you result in the number 666, an Unholy Trinity. The book of The Revelation speaks of this Unholy Trinity in the form of Satan, the Antichrist, and the Beast. Satan even heals the Antichrist from an apparently fatal wound in imitation of Jesus' death and resurrection. Then the Antichrist rules a new Gentile world order characterized by wealth, greed, selfishness, ambition, pleasure, and power. Combined with idolatry, these characteristics could be said to apply to King Solomon's empire as described above. They might also be used to describe the current world conditions. Thus, one conclusion you can make is that the number 666 applies to an Unholy Trinity worshipped by the Gentile world.

But there is even more to the number 666. The scripture above that describes the mark of the Beast states that no one will be able to get a job or shop in any store without receiving the mark of the Beast on the right hand or the forehead. Much has been made of this prophecy. Some have equated the value 666 to the numeric value of various descriptors of the Romans, who ruled when The Revelation was written. Many have tried to take the names of current political figures and, applying numeric codes to the letters, derive the number 666. Others have equated the number to the social security system, which requires a number for employment and retirement benefits. Still others have equated it to the information highway which interconnects individuals, financial institutions, and even countries in a way never before seen in the world's history. While some of the elements of these theories may play a role in the environment at the end of time, none of them explain the mark of the Beast.

Though much has been made of the mark of the Beast, little has been made of the Seal of God. As you saw above in the study of the number 144 (1 + 4 + 4 = 9), the Seal of God will be placed on the foreheads of 144,000 of his believers at the end of time. Yet no one is developing extravagant theories to define what the Seal of God will look like as it is placed on people's foreheads. It is unlikely that either the Seal of God or the mark of the Beast are literally to be applied to people's foreheads or hands. It is much more likely that this description is a symbolic representation of what is to occur. You have already taken a preliminary look at the mark of the Beast, 666. Take a quick look at what might be considered its opposite, the Seal of God:

... Seal of God ... (The Revelation 9:4)

σφραγιδα του θεου

Implicit Value = 200 + 500 + 100 + 1 + 3 + 10 + 4 + 1 + 300 + 70 + 400 + 9 + 5 + 70 + 400 = 2073

2 + 0 + 7 + 3 = 12

1 + 2 = 3

The implicit value of the Seal of God is equivalent to the number that symbolizes the Holy Trinity and actions thereof. The Seal of God placed on the foreheads represents them as followers of the Holy Trinity. You can recognize them as followers because their thoughts and actions revolve around their faith.

So to get back to the mark of the Beast, put together what you learned from the book of The Revelation, have learned from your study of the numbers of the Bible, and your review of the kingdom of Solomon when the same number also appeared in scripture. At the end of time, an Unholy Trinity will rule a new world order that worships wealth, greed, materialism, and worldly pleasures as if they were gods. In fact, these worldly characteristics are probably taken even far beyond where they are today, to the point that a visitor to this world might report that the earth's inhabitants worshipped these characteristics as idols.

This state of affairs would most certainly create an environment in which discrimination against anyone who did not have the same views would exist. Denying employment and/or service are two traditional forms of discrimination. It is likely, therefore, that the forehead and hand are symbols of thoughts and actions. The mark of the beast on the forehead and hand symbolizes that you will know the followers of the Unholy Trinity by the evidence of their worship of materialism as if it was divine.

As a conclusion to this discussion of the mark of the Beast, let's review a few implicit uses of the number 666. As you saw with the number 144, the number 666 possesses the property that no matter what number you multiply it by, the result is a number with digits that add to the number *nine*. For example, 666 * 15 = 9990, 9 + 9 + 9 = 27, 2 + 7 = 9. The implicit value of 666 appears just where you would expect:

... the kingdoms of the world ... (Luke 4:5)

βασιλειας οικουμενης

Implicit Value = 2 + 1 + 200 + 10 + 30 + 5 + 10 + 1 + 200 + 70 + 10 + 20 + 70 + 400 + 40 + 5 + 50 + 8 + 200 = 1332

1332 = *666* * 2

... businessmen throughout the world ... (The Revelation 18:3)

οι εμποροι γης

Implicit Value = 70 + 10 + 5 + 40 + 80 + 70 + 100 + 70 + 10 + 3 + 8 + 200 = *666*

... profit. (Ecclesiastes 10:11)

יתרון

Implicit Value = 10 + 400 + 200 + 6 + 50 = *666*

The Number and Implicit Value—999

You might think with the analysis of the number 666 I have come to the end of the analysis of God's numeric code, but I have one final number to briefly review. It is a number very appropriate to this chapter, and its simplicity is a testament to the miracle of the numeric code of the Bible. If you multiply the foundation number of 111 by *nine*, you get 999 (9 + 9 + 9 = 27, 2 + 7 = 9). 999 is a very interesting number because it is the product of a number symbolizing the Holy Trinity and the number representing the end, and when you add the individual digits together, you come back to the number *nine*. It symbolizes the final judgment. Look at a few examples:

But instead, you will be brought down to the pit of hell.... (Isaiah 14:15)

אך אל שאול תורר

Implicit Value = 1 + 20 + 1 + 30 + 300 + 1 + 6 + 30 + 400 + 6 + 200 + 4 = **999**

... my wrath ... (Hebrews 4:3)

τη οργη μου

Implicit Value = 300 + 8 + 70 + 100 + 3 + 8 + 40 + 70 + 400 = **999**

But the meek shall inherit the earth ... (Psalms 37:11)

ועניים יירשו ארץ

Implicit Value = 6 + 70 + 50 + 6 + 10 + 40 + 10 + 10 + 200 + 300 + 6 + 1 + 200 + 90 = **999**

Summary

The number *nine* is the final number in the divine numeric code of the Bible. Therefore, it is logical that it should represent what brings things to an end. The symbolism of the number *nine* is summarized below:

- End of a state of being

- End of life

- The end of time

You also learned how the number 144 (1 + 4 + 4 = **9**) is a significant number on its own right and not just an amplification of the number

12 (1 + 2 = 3). It represents the chosen at the end of time. And with your knowledge of the numbers *three*, *six*, and *nine*, you have solved the puzzle of the number 666 (6 + 6 + 6 = 18, 1 + 8 = 9), the mark of the Beast. The number 666 represents the Unholy Trinity of Satan, the Antichrist, and the Beast. They will rule the world at the end of time when the people of the carnal world will worship materialism as if it were divine.

Summing It All Up

The numbers in the Bible do not occur randomly. They follow a specific code of symbolism that adds more depth and meaning to the associated scriptures. By this statement, I do not mean to imply that every number appearing in the Bible adheres to this divine code. Many numbers are simply counts or ranks. But it is amazing how many numbers in the Bible do carry this code, and every significant number adheres to it.

In contrast to the approach used in the Bible, take your local newspaper. Do you have a newspaper available to you? If so, read several articles by different writers in different sections of the newspaper and make note of the numbers you come across. Do the same numbers appear repeatedly in the same contexts? Do they seem to be telling you more than the count or rank of their subjects? Of course not. But in the Bible, that is exactly what happens.

The message of the previous chapters has developed your capability to interpret the symbolism of the numbers of the Bible. Through weight of evidence and presentation of logical connectors, this book has proved that the Bible, though physically written by many men with varied backgrounds, really had one author and that author was God. I hope by now that the sheer number of examples and related supporting evidence has overwhelmed even the most obstinate doubters.

I have shown you how to take a number with more than one digit and reduce it to a single digit through repeated addition of the digits. I have also shown how you can take the written word and convert it to a number by assigning each letter the appropriate numeric value from the ancient numbering systems. Whether a number in the Bible occurs explicitly in scripture or is derived implicitly from the letters in the words, it contains the same symbolism.

Chapter by chapter, I have described the logical manner in which each number builds on the symbolism of its predecessor to establish a new meaning. There are only *nine* numbers in the divine code and their meanings are easy to understand. God does not mean this system to be so complex that only a few learned people can comprehend it. He means it to be simple and easily understood.

The table below shows the progression of the numbers of the Bible in summary fashion. It also indicates the logical grouping into *three* sets of *three* numbers. What else should you expect by now but that the numeric code of the Bible would be grouped into *threes* since it represents such a miraculous act of God?

Progression of the Numeric Code of the Bible

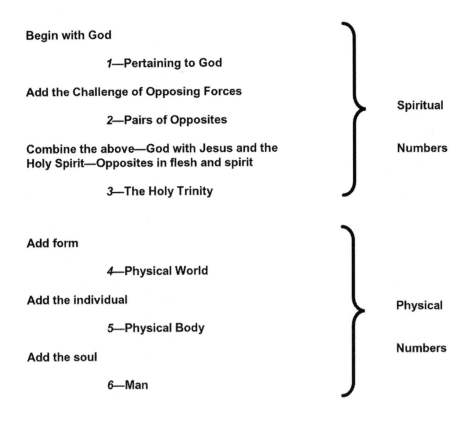

Begin with God

       1—Pertaining to God

Add the Challenge of Opposing Forces

       2—Pairs of Opposites

Combine the above—God with Jesus and the Holy Spirit—Opposites in flesh and spirit

       3—The Holy Trinity

} **Spiritual Numbers**

Add form

       4—Physical World

Add the individual

       5—Physical Body

Add the soul

       6—Man

} **Physical Numbers**

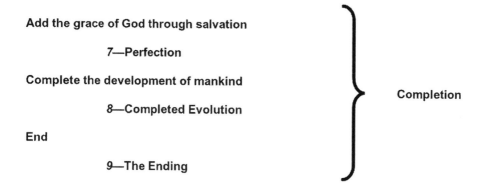

Add the grace of God through salvation

7—Perfection

Complete the development of mankind

8—Completed Evolution

End

9—The Ending

Completion

Having reviewed the progression of the numeric code, I wish now to review the symbolism of each number as presented in the preceding chapters:

Symbolism of the Numeric Code of the Bible

One—Pertaining to God

- The *one* God omnipresent.

- Items with a direct relationship to God.

- Relationship of the individual with God

- Relationship of God with his church.

Two—Pairs of Opposites

- God and the world

- Good and evil

- Male and female

- Righteous and unrighteous

- Right and wrong

- Old Testament Law and New Testament grace

- Rivals

Three—The Holy Trinity

- Pertaining to the Holy Trinity

- Acts of God—especially involving Jesus or the Holy Spirit

- Age to begin God's service

- Association with Jesus

- Path to salvation

- God's chosen from the masses (demonstrated through the number 12)

Four—Physical World

- Physical aspects of God

- Physical tests

- Punishment on the world or the chosen people

- Entire world

- Worldly kingdoms

- Worldly service

Five—Physical Body

- The body

- The senses

- Physical desires

- Miracles

- Overcoming constraints of nature

- Offspring and generations

- Physical injury

- Physical appearance of Jesus following death and resurrection

Six—Man

- Imperfection of man

- Sin

- Satan's influence

- Other angels

- Evil kingdoms

- The man who overcame the physical world and the salvation available to his followers

Seven—Perfection

- Achievement of perfection

- Making holy

- Setting apart as sacred

- Consecration

- Fulfillment of prophecy

- Opposites of the above, such as the Antichrist and fall from grace

Eight—Completed Evolution

- Achievement of completion

- Faith

- Fulfillment of intent

- Chosen people

- Resurrection

- Jesus as the ultimate man

Nine—The Ending

- End of a state of being

- End of life

- The end of time

And finally, review the implicit value chain that I built from chapter to chapter:

Implicit Value	Multiplier	Associated Meaning
37		The perfect act of God in sending his Son Jesus to earth
111	*37 * 3*	The Holy Trinity and related acts
666	*111 * 6*	The Unholy Trinity and the worship of materialism
777	*111 * 7*	Precious, perfect acts of God
888	*111 * 8*	Jesus Christ—the ultimate man
999	*111 * 9*	Final judgment

The above numeric code adds a new dimension to the word of God as written in the scriptures of the Bible. Understanding of this additional dimension is a lost art. In today's environment, with its emphasis on the superficial and form over substance, perhaps this loss should be understandable. But accepting this loss robs God's followers of the reward associated with complete comprehension of his word. That reward is what is offered the true disciple of the Bible. It is the difference between *reading* the scripture and *comprehending* the scripture.

Take a simple example.

> 1 Kings 10:18 Solomon also made a huge ivory throne and overlaid it with pure gold. It had *six* steps and a rounded back, with arm rests; and a lion standing on each side. And there were two lions on each step—*twelve* in all. There was no other throne in all the world so splendid as that one. (1 Kings 10:18)

The casual reader of this scripture would focus on the splendor and opulence of this throne—*ivory overlaid with pure gold*. Wow! What a throne! How wealthy King Solomon must have been, and how great his empire! But by focusing on this aspect of the scripture, you would lose another level of understanding embedded in the numbers.

King Solomon designed his throne with *six* steps to represent his longing for perfection. Why *six* and not *seven*? Because King Solomon was wise enough to know that, no matter how much he longed for it, he could not achieve perfection. He also put *twelve* lions on the steps of his throne. King Solomon knew he ruled the chosen people of God only because God had chosen him to do so. If he had maintained this belief, his descendants would not have lost that same throne to outsiders. What a difference understanding the keys to the numeric code of the Bible makes for the reader!

With this book, I have just tapped the surface of the messages you can draw from the numbers of the Bible. There are many subtleties in the numeric code that I have only briefly explored in this short discourse. For example, I have noted only a few instances of the additional meanings associated with interim results that occur when reducing large numbers to a single digit. But these subtle differences do exist. An example may make this thought more clear. The number 1656 reduces to 18 before being reduced to the number *nine* (1656, $1 + 6 + 5 + 6 = 18$, $1 + 8 = 9$). The number 1998 reduces to 27 before being reduced to the number *nine* (1998, $1 + 9 + 9 + 8 = 27$, $2 + 7 = 9$). Both of these numbers reduce to the number *nine*, but since they reduce to different two-digit numbers in the earlier state, they have subtle differences in meaning.

Similarly, many other subtleties within the numeric code exist but cannot be included here. Anyone who is interested in pursuing this subject further should do so. The reward for delving more deeply into this subject will be immense. In no way does this book attempt to contain all of the examples where a number in the Bible carries with it a symbolic meaning beyond the number itself. Please take the time to read the scriptures, find additional examples, and experience the richness for yourself.

Appendix A

The Names of God

Overview

Consistent with the discussion above about how the numeric code of the Bible adds meaning to words in the Bible, the name of God in Hebrew is not a generic title but has additional meaning. In ancient Hebrew a name carried a connotation that passed along the essence of the person named. There are many Hebrew names of God used in the Bible, and each name carries with it a meaning that gives insight into who God is. And as you have learned, since the names are composed of letters and letters are used as numbers, you can assign numeric values to the names. The numeric values provide you with even more depth of meaning.

In the sections below, I will describe some of the names of God that appear in the Bible. Following the description, I will provide the name in Hebrew and compute the numeric value.

Yahweh (Jehovah)

The most important of God's names is the four-letter name YHVH. It is equivalent to the name Jehovah, which was a mistaken translation that nevertheless has continued in use. It has as its source the Hebrew root for *to be*, and means *he is* or *he lives*. It relates to God's conversation with Moses in which God calls himself, *I Am Who I Am*, also translated as *I Am He Who Is* or *I Shall Be Who I Shall Be*. Strictly speaking it is the only proper name of God. The connotation is that God is eternal. Yahweh is the living God. He is not a lifeless idol as was worshipped by the pagan Gentiles. God reveals himself to man unceasingly.

Historically, the name Yahweh has often been referred to as *The Name*, or *The Unutterable Name*. In scripture it is often used when God is interacting with humans. It appears 6823 (6 + 8 + 2 + 3 = 19, 1 + 0 = *1*) times in the Old Testament. The written name Yahweh was only spoken out loud by the priests in the Temple when blessing the people. It was never used outside of the Temple.

The implicit value of Yahweh resolves to *eight*, which you know to symbolize the ultimate evolution:

Yahweh, or Jehovah

יהוה

Implicit Value = 10 + 5 + 6 + 5 = 26

2 + 6 = *8*

The name Yahweh is often combined with other names to reveal additional aspects of God's character. Some of those names are:

Yahweh Yireh: The Lord Will Provide
(God will always provide for his people.)

יהוה יראה

Implicit Value = 10 + 5 + 6 + 5 + 10 + 200 + 1 + 5 = 242

2 + 4 + 2 = *8*

Yahweh Mekoddishkem: The Lord Who Sets Apart
(God sets apart his chosen people. By this act, they are consecrated as belonging to God and are given special care.)

יהוה קדש

Implicit Value = 10 + 5 + 6 + 5 + 100 + 4 + 300 = 430

$$4 + 3 + 0 = 7$$

Yahweh Rophe: The Lord Who Heals
(God heals physically and spiritually.)

יהוה רפא

Implicit Value = $10 + 5 + 6 + 5 + 200 + 1 + 80 = 307$

$$3 + 0 + 7 = 10$$

$$1 + 0 = 1$$

Yahweh Nissi: The Lord Our Banner
(God lifts up his people and fights for them. He is their focal point during their trials and tribulations.)

יהוה נסי

Implicit Value = $10 + 5 + 6 + 5 + 50 + 60 + 10 = 146$

$$1 + 4 + 6 = 11$$

$$1 + 1 = 2$$

Yahweh Shalom: The Lord Our Peace
(God brings harmony and fulfillment and restores relationships.)

יהוה שלום

Implicit Value = $10 + 5 + 6 + 5 + 300 + 30 + 6 + 40 = 402$

$$4 + 0 + 2 = 6$$

Yahweh Tsidkenu: The Lord Our Righteousness
(God is the means to righteousness.)

יהוה צדכנו

Implicit Value = 10 + 5 + 6 + 5 + 90 + 4 + 20 + 50 + 6 = 196

1 + 9 + 6 = 16

1 + 6 = **7**

Yahweh Rohi: The Lord Our Shepherd
(God cares for his people as they go out in the world as a shepherd would for his sheep or as a friend would do for another.)

יהוה רעה

Implicit Value = 10 + 5 + 6 + 5 + 200 + 70 + 5 = 301

3 + 0 + 1 = **4**

Yahweh Shammah: The Lord is There
(God is eternally present.)

יהוה שמה

Implicit Value = 10 + 5 + 6 + 5 + 300 + 40 + 5 = 371

3 + 7 + 1 = 11

1 + 1 = **2**

Yahweh Sabaoth: The Lord of Hosts
(God is the commander of the armies of heaven.)

יהוה צבא

Implicit Value = 10 + 5 + 6 + 5 + 90 + 2 + 1 = 119

$$1 + 1 + 9 = 11$$

$$1 + 1 = 2$$

Yahweh Elohim: The Lord God
(The Lord is the true God of the world, not the idols or other false gods worshipped by many.)

יהוה אלהים

$$\text{Implicit Value} = 10 + 5 + 6 + 5 + 1 + 30 + 5 + 10 + 40 = 112$$

$$1 + 1 + 2 = 4$$

Elohim

The common name of God is Elohim. It is the first name used for God in the Bible and is used 2357 times ($2 + 3 + 5 + 7 = 17, 1 + 7 = 8$). It is the plural form of the word El and/or the feminine word Eloha. It is the same name of God as Elah in Aramaic and Allah (from the compound word *Al-ilah*, which means *the God*) in Arabic. Though it is a plural word it is used with singular verbs, similar to the concepts of the Holy Trinity being viewed as a single entity or a ruler using the royal *we* when referring to himself/herself. In one sense Elohim simply means *god* and is also used in singular and plural form for pagan gods, though with a plural verb when used for pagan gods. In another sense it connotes great power and is an expression of God's sovereignty over man.

The implicit value of Elohim resolves to *five* because it gives physical form and characteristics to the otherwise unfathomable nature and actions of God:

Elohim

אלהים

$$\text{Implicit Value} = 1 + 30 + 5 + 10 + 40 = 86$$

$$8 + 6 = 14$$

$$1 + 4 = 5$$

Coincidentally, the word *nature* has the same implicit value:

הסבים

Implicit Value $= 5 + 2 + 9 + 10 + 60 = 86$

$$8 + 6 = 14$$

$$1 + 4 = 5$$

Like the name Yahweh, El is often combined with other names to reveal additional aspects of God's character. Examples of those names include:

El Shaddai: God with overpowering strength
(God all powerful and to be feared.)

אל שדי

Implicit Value $= 1 + 30 + 300 + 4 + 10 = 345$

$$3 + 4 + 5 = 12$$

$$1 + 2 = 3$$

El Elyon: God most high
(God is the supreme sovereign.)

אל עליון

Implicit Value $= 1 + 30 + 70 + 30 + 10 + 6 + 50 = 197$

$$1 + 9 + 7 = 17$$

$$1 + 7 = 8$$

El Olam: God everlasting
(God has existed forever and will exist forever.)

אל עולם

Implicit Value = $1 + 30 + 70 + 6 + 30 + 40 = 177$

$$1 + 7 + 7 = 15$$

$$1 + 5 = 6$$

El Echad: The *one* God
(There is only *one* God and no other.)

אל אחד

Implicit Value = $1 + 30 + 1 + 8 + 4 = 44$

$$4 + 4 = 8$$

El Hanneeman: Faithful God
(God fulfills his promises to his people.)

אל הנאמן

Implicit Value = $1 + 30 + 5 + 50 + 1 + 40 + 50 = 177$

$$1 + 7 + 7 = 15$$

$$1 + 5 = 6$$

El Emet: God of Truth
(God keeps his word.)

אל אמת

Implicit Value = 1 + 30 + 1 + 40 + 400 = 472

$$4 + 7 + 2 = 13$$

$$1 + 3 = 4$$

El Kanno: Jealous God
(God watches his people closely.)

אל קנוא

Implicit Value = 1 + 30 + 100 + 50 + 6 + 1 = 188

$$1 + 8 + 8 = 17$$

$$1 + 7 = 8$$

El Hakodosh: Holy God
(God is unique, one of a kind, and sacred.)

אל הקדוש

Implicit Value = 1 + 30 + 5 + 100 + 4 + 6 + 300 = 446

$$4 + 4 + 6 = 14$$

$$1 + 4 = 5$$

Adonai

As indicated above, the written name Yahweh was only spoken out loud by the priests in the Temple when blessing the people. It was never used outside of the Temple. There was no scriptural prohibition against speaking the name out loud, but speaking the name in the wrong context or situation could bring the charge of blasphemy and death. Fear of this charge and punishment led to a sort of common law prohibition against speaking the name outside of the Temple. In fact, since the Temple was destroyed in the first century and the name was never spoken outside the Temple, the correct pronunciation was eventually lost and is not now known with certainty. Vowels were not written in ancient Hebrew and were supplied by the reader.

To get around the prohibition against speaking the name, the name Adonai began to be substituted. Adoni is singular and refers to a superior or *my lord*. When used as a substitute for the name Yahweh, the plural form of the word is used—Adonai. Therefore, similarly to Elohim, Adonai is a plural word used in the singular form as a name for God. The singular form of the word is used 195 (1 + 9 + 5 = 15, 1 + 5 = 6) times in the Bible in relation to a superior who is not God. It is used 149 (4 + 4 + 9 = 17, 1 + 7 = 8) times in the plural form to refer to God.

> **Adonai**: My Lord
> (Denotes God's position and authority.)
>
> אדני
>
> Implicit Value = 1 + 4 + 50 + 10 = 65
>
> 6 + 5 = 11
>
> 1 + 1 = 2

There are other less common names of God that I will not go into here. There are also many descriptive titles, a few of which are listed below:

Judge

שפע

Implicit Value = 300 + 80 + 70 = 450

4 + 5 + 0 = **9**

Branch

צמח

Implicit Value = 90 + 40 + 8 = 138

1 + 3 + 8 = 12

1 + 2 = **3**

Deliverer

פלע

Implicit Value = 80 + 30 + 70 = 180

1 + 8 + 0 = **9**

Redeemer

גאל

Implicit Value = 3 + 1 + 30 = 34

3 + 4 = **7**

King

מלך

Implicit Value = 30 + 40 + 20 = 90

$9 + 0 = 9$

Appendix B

The 613 Commandments of the Torah

Everyone is aware of the **Ten** Commandments, but few are aware that there are 613 (6 + 1 + 3 = 10, 1 + 0 = *1*) commandments in the Torah. These commandments together are known as the *mitzvot*, or *taryag mitzvot*, with *taryag* representing a pronunciation of the letters that make up the number 613. Ancient Hebrews lived there life according to these laws, not just the **Ten** Commandments.

The Hebrew word for law is *Torah*, but it really means *to teach or instruct*. Mitzvot is the Hebrew word for commandments. While the Torah is often thought to refer to the Pentateuch, the first five books of the Old Testament attributed to Moses, it also refers to the entire Old Testament. When Paul refers to the Law in his letters, he is referring to the mitzvot. To the Hebrews, the Law represented the revealed mind of God. It was given to man for his protection and good fortune. Since it came from God, it was itself divine, and to speak against the Law was to speak against God. Amazingly the implicit value of the Hebrew letters in *Moses Our Teacher*, the name and title by which Moses is known to this day, also equals 613.

The 613 mitzvot are made up of 248 (2 + 4 + 8 = 14, 1 + 4 = 5) positive commandments and 365 (3 + 6 + 5 = 14, 1 + 4 = 5) negative commandments. 248 at the time was believed to be the number of bones and significant organs in the human body, and 365 corresponded to the number of days in a year. The mitzvot cover all aspects of human life from spirituality to ceremony, to treatment of Hebrews and Gentiles, to family, to sex, to diet, to business practices, to legal procedures, to the Temple and priesthood, to war, and many other areas.

The following list contains the 613 mitzvot and their source in scripture, as enumerated by the 12th century rabbi Moses Maimonides in his most renowned literary work, *Mishneh Torah*.

1. To know there is a God (Exodus 20:2)
2. Not to entertain thoughts of other gods besides him (Exodus 20:3)
3. To know that he is *one* (Deuteronomy 6:4)
4. To love him (Deuteronomy 6:5)
5. To fear him (Deuteronomy 10:20)
6. To sanctify his name (Leviticus 22:32)
7. Not to profane his name (Leviticus 22:32)
8. Not to destroy objects associated with his name (Deuteronomy 12:4)
9. To listen to the prophet speaking in his name (Deuteronomy 18:15)
10. Not to test the prophet unduly (Deuteronomy 6:16)
11. To emulate his ways (Deuteronomy 28:9)
12. To cleave to those who know him (Deuteronomy 10:20)
13. To love other Jews (Leviticus 19:18)
14. To love converts (Deuteronomy 10:19)
15. Not to hate fellow Jews (Leviticus 19:17)
16. To reprove a sinner (Leviticus 19:17)
17. Not to embarrass others (Leviticus 19:17)
18. Not to oppress the weak (Exodus 22:21)
19. Not to speak derogatorily of others (Leviticus 19:16)
20. Not to take revenge (Leviticus 19:18)
21. Not to bear a grudge (Leviticus 19:18)
22. To learn Torah (Deuteronomy 6:7)
23. To honor those who teach and know Torah (Leviticus 19:32)
24. Not to inquire into idolatry (Leviticus 19:4)
25. Not to follow the whims of your heart or what your eyes see (Numbers 15:39)
26. Not to blaspheme (Exodus 22:27)
27. Not to worship idols in the manner they are worshiped (Exodus 20:5)
28. Not to worship idols in the *four* ways we worship God (Exodus 20:5)
29. Not to make an idol for yourself (Exodus 20:4)
30. Not to make an idol for others (Leviticus 19:4)
31. Not to make human forms even for decorative purposes (Exodus 20:20)
32. Not to turn a city to idolatry (Exodus 23:13)
33. To burn a city that has turned to idol worship (Deuteronomy 13:17)
34. Not to rebuild it as a city (Deuteronomy 13:17)

35. Not to derive benefit from it (Deuteronomy 13:18)
36. Not to missionize an individual to idol worship (Deuteronomy 13:12)
37. Not to love the missionary (Deuteronomy 13:9)
39. Not to save the missionary (Deuteronomy 13:9)
40. Not to say anything in his defense (Deuteronomy 13:9)
41. Not to refrain from incriminating him (Deuteronomy 13:9)
42. Not to prophesize in the name of idolatry (Deuteronomy 13:14)
43. Not to listen to a false prophet (Deuteronomy 13:4)
44. Not to prophesize falsely in the name of God (Deuteronomy 18:20)
45. Not to be afraid of killing the false prophet (Deuteronomy 18:22)
46. Not to swear in the name of an idol (Exodus 23:13)
47. Not to perform ov (medium) (Leviticus 19:31)
48. Not to perform yidoni ("magical seer") (Leviticus 19:31)
49. Not to pass your children through the fire to Molech (Leviticus 18:21)
50. Not to erect a column in a public place of worship (Deuteronomy 16:22)
51. Not to bow down on smooth stone (Leviticus 26:1)
52. Not to plant a tree in the Temple courtyard (Deuteronomy 16:21)
53. To destroy idols and their accessories (Deuteronomy 12:2)
54. Not to derive benefit from idols and their accessories (Deuteronomy 7:26)
55. Not to derive benefit from ornaments of idols (Deuteronomy 7:25)
56. Not to make a covenant with idolaters (Deuteronomy 7:2)
57. Not to show favor to them (Deuteronomy 7:2)
58. Not to let them dwell in the land of Israel (Exodus 23:33)
59. Not to imitate them in customs and clothing (Leviticus 20:23)
60. Not to be superstitious (Leviticus 19:26)
61. Not to go into a trance to foresee events, etc. (Deuteronomy 18:10)
62. Not to engage in astrology (Leviticus 19:26)
63. Not to mutter incantations (Deuteronomy 18:11)
64. Not to attempt to contact the dead (Deuteronomy 18:11)
65. Not to consult the ov (Deuteronomy 18:11)
66. Not to consult the yidoni (Deuteronomy 18:11)
67. Not to perform acts of magic (Deuteronomy 18:10)
68. Men must not shave the hair off the sides of their head (Leviticus 19:27)
69. Men must not shave their beards with a razor (Leviticus 19:27)

70. Men must not wear women's clothing (Deuteronomy 22:5)
71. Women must not wear men's clothing (Deuteronomy 22:5)
72. Not to tattoo the skin (Leviticus 19:28)
73. Not to tear the skin in mourning (Deuteronomy 14:1)
74. Not to make a bald spot in mourning (Deuteronomy 14:1)
75. To repent and confess wrongdoings (Numbers 5:7)
76. To say the Shema twice daily (Deuteronomy 6:7)
77. To serve the Almighty with prayer daily (Exodus 23:25)
78. The Kohanim must bless the Jewish nation daily (Numbers 6:23)
79. To wear tefillin (phylacteries) on the head (Deuteronomy 6:8)
80. To bind tefillin on the arm (Deuteronomy 6:8)
81. To put a mezuzah on each door post (Deuteronomy 6:9)
82. Each male must write a Torah scroll (Deuteronomy 31:19)
83. The king must have a separate Sefer Torah for himself (Deuteronomy 17:18)
84. To have tzitzit on *four*-cornered garments (Numbers 15:38)
85. To bless the Almighty after eating (Deuteronomy 8:10)
86. To circumcise all males on the *eighth* day after their birth (Leviticus 12:3)
87. To rest on the *seventh* day (Exodus 23:12
88. Not to do prohibited labor on the seventh day (Exodus 20:10)
89. The court must not inflict punishment on Shabbat (Exodus 35:3)
90. Not to walk outside the city boundary on Shabbat (Exodus 16:29)
91. To sanctify the day with Kiddush and Havdalah (Exodus 20:8)
92. To rest from prohibited labor (Leviticus 23:32)
93. Not to do prohibited labor on Yom Kippur (Leviticus 23:32)
94. To afflict yourself on Yom Kippur (Leviticus 16:29)
95. Not to eat or drink on Yom Kippur (Leviticus 23:29)
96. To rest on the first day of Passover (Leviticus 23:7)
97. Not to do prohibited labor on the first day of Passover (Leviticus 23:8)
98. To rest on the *seventh* day of Passover (Leviticus 23:8)
99. Not to do prohibited labor on the *seventh* day of Passover (Leviticus 23:8)
100. To rest on Shavuot (Leviticus 23:21)
101. Not to do prohibited labor on Shavuot (Leviticus 23:21)
102. To rest on Rosh Hashana (Leviticus 23:24)

103. Not to do prohibited labor on Rosh Hashana (Leviticus 23:25)
104. To rest on Sukkot (Leviticus 23:35)
105. Not to do prohibited labor on Sukkot (Leviticus 23:35)
106. To rest on Shmini Atzeret (Leviticus 23:36)
107. Not to do prohibited labor on Shmini Atzeret (Leviticus 23:36)
108. Not to eat chametz on the afternoon of the 14th day of Nissan (Deuteronomy 16:3)
109. To destroy all chametz on 14th day of Nissan (Exodus 12:15)
110. Not to eat chametz all *seven* days of Passover (Exodus 13:3)
111. Not to eat mixtures containing chametz all *seven* days of Passover (Exodus 12:20)
112. Not to see chametz in your domain *seven* days (Exodus 13:7)
113. Not to find chametz in your domain *seven* days (Exodus 12:19)
114. To eat matzah on the first night of Passover (Exodus 12:18)
115. To relate the Exodus from Egypt on that night (Exodus 13:8)
116. To hear the Shofar on the first day of Tishrei (Rosh Hashana) (Numbers 9:1)
117. To dwell in a Sukkah for the *seven* days of Sukkot (Leviticus 23:42)
118. To take up a Lulav and Etrog all *seven* days (Leviticus 23:40)
119. Each man must give a half shekel annually (Exodus 30:13)
120. Courts must calculate to determine when a new month begins (Exodus 12:2)
121. To afflict and cry out before God in times of catastrophe (Numbers 10:9)
122. To marry a wife by means of ketubah and kiddushin (Deuteronomy 22:13)
123. Not to have sexual relations with women not thus married (Deuteronomy 23:18)
124. Not to withhold food, clothing, and sexual relations from your wife (Exodus 21:10)
125. To have children with one's wife (Genesis 1:28)
126. To issue a divorce by means of a Get document (Deuteronomy 24:1)
127. A man must not remarry his wife after she has married someone else (Deuteronomy 24:4)
128. To do yibbum (marry the widow of one's childless brother) (Deuteronomy 25:5)

129. To do chalitzah (free the widow of one's childless brother from yibbum) (Deuteronomy 25:9)
130. The widow must not remarry until the ties with her brother-in-law are removed (Deuteronomy 25:5)
131. The court must fine one who sexually seduces a maiden (Exodus 22:15-16)
132. The rapist must marry the maiden (if she chooses) (Deuteronomy 22:29)
133. He is never allowed to divorce her (Deuteronomy 22:29)
134. The slanderer must remain married to his wife (Deuteronomy 22:19)
135. He must not divorce her (Deuteronomy 22:19)
136. To fulfill the laws of the Sotah (Numbers 5:30)
137. Not to put oil on her meal offering (Numbers 5:15)
138. Not to put frankincense on her meal offering (Numbers 5:15)
139. Not to have sexual relations with your mother (Leviticus 18:7)
140. Not to have sexual relations with your father's wife (Leviticus 18:8)
141. Not to have sexual relations with your sister (Leviticus 18:9)
142. Not to have sexual relations with your father's wife's daughter (Leviticus 18:11)
143. Not to have sexual relations with your son's daughter (Leviticus 18:10)
144. Not to have sexual relations with your daughter (Leviticus 18:6, Leviticus 18:10)
145. Not to have sexual relations with your daughter's daughter (Leviticus 18:10)
146. Not to have sexual relations with a woman and her daughter (Leviticus 18:17)
147. Not to have sexual relations with a woman and her son's daughter (Leviticus 18:17)
148. Not to have sexual relations with a woman and her daughter's daughter (Leviticus 18:17)
149. Not to have sexual relations with your father's sister (Leviticus 18:12)
150. Not to have sexual relations with your mother's sister (Leviticus 18:13)

151. Not to have sexual relations with your father's brother's wife (Leviticus 18:14)
152. Not to have sexual relations with your son's wife (Leviticus 18:15)
153. Not to have sexual relations with your brother's wife (Leviticus 18:16)
154. Not to have sexual relations with your wife's sister (Leviticus 18:18)
155. A man must not have sexual relations with a beast (Leviticus 18:23)
156. A woman must not have sexual relations with a beast (Leviticus 18:23)
157. Not to have homosexual sexual relations (Leviticus 18:22)
158. Not to have homosexual sexual relations with your father (Leviticus 18:7)
159. Not to have homosexual sexual relations with your father's brother (Leviticus 18:14)
160. Not to have sexual relations with someone else's wife (Leviticus 18:20)
161. Not to have sexual relations with a menstrually impure woman (Leviticus 18:19)
162. Not to marry non-Jews (Deuteronomy 7:3)
163. Not to let Moabite and Ammonite males marry into the Jewish people (Deuteronomy 23:4)
164. Don't keep a third-generation Egyptian convert from marrying into the Jewish people (Deuteronomy 23:8-9)
165. Not to refrain from marrying a third generation Edomite convert (Deuteronomy 23:8-9)
166. Not to let a mamzer (a child born due to an illegal relationship) marry into the Jewish people (Deuteronomy 23:3)
167. Not to let a eunuch marry into the Jewish people (Deuteronomy 23:2)
168. Not to offer to God any castrated male animals (Leviticus 22:24)
169. The High Priest must not marry a widow (Leviticus 21:14)
170. The High Priest must not have sexual relations with a widow even outside of marriage (Leviticus 21:15)
171. The High Priest must marry a virgin maiden (Leviticus 21:13)
172. A Kohen (priest) must not marry a divorcee (Leviticus 21:7)

173. A Kohen must not marry a zonah (a woman who has had a forbidden sexual relationship) (Leviticus 21:7)
174. A priest must not marry a chalalah ("a desecrated person") (party to or product of 169-172) (Leviticus 21:7)
175. Not to make pleasurable (sexual) contact with any forbidden woman (Leviticus 18:6)
176. To examine the signs of animals to distinguish between kosher and non-kosher (Leviticus 11:2)
177. To examine the signs of fowl to distinguish between kosher and non-kosher (Deuteronomy 14:11)
178. To examine the signs of fish to distinguish between kosher and non-kosher (Leviticus 11:9)
179. To examine the signs of locusts to distinguish between kosher and non-kosher (Leviticus 11:21)
180. Not to eat non-kosher animals (Leviticus 11:4)
181. Not to eat non-kosher fowl (Leviticus 11:13)
182. Not to eat non-kosher fish (Leviticus 11:11)
183. Not to eat non-kosher flying insects (Deuteronomy 14:19)
184. Not to eat non-kosher creatures that crawl on land (Leviticus 11:41)
185. Not to eat non-kosher maggots (Leviticus 11:44)
186. Not to eat worms found in fruit on the ground (Leviticus 11:42)
187. Not to eat creatures that live in water other than (kosher) fish (Leviticus 11:43)
188. Not to eat the meat of an animal that died without ritual slaughter (Deuteronomy 14:21)
189. Not to benefit from an ox condemned to be stoned (Exodus 21:28)
190. Not to eat meat of an animal that was mortally wounded (Exodus 22:30)
191. Not to eat a limb torn off a living creature (Deuteronomy 12:23)
192. Not to eat blood (Leviticus 3:17)
193. Not to eat certain fats of clean animals (Leviticus 3:17)
194. Not to eat the sinew of the thigh (Genesis 32:33)
195. Not to eat meat and milk cooked together (Exodus 23:19)
196. Not to cook meat and milk together (Exodus 34:26)
197. Not to eat bread from new grain before the Omer (Leviticus 23:14)
198. Not to eat parched grains from new grain before the Omer (Leviticus 23:14)

199. Not to eat ripened grains from new grain before the Omer (Leviticus 23:14)
200. Not to eat fruit of a tree during its first *three* years (Leviticus 19:23)
201. Not to eat diverse seeds planted in a vineyard (Deuteronomy 22:9)
202. Not to eat untithed fruits (Leviticus 22:15)
203. Not to drink wine poured in service to idols (Deuteronomy 32:38)
204. To ritually slaughter an animal before eating it (Deuteronomy 12:21)
205. Not to slaughter an animal and its offspring on the same day (Leviticus 22:28)
206. To cover the blood (of a slaughtered beast or fowl) with earth (Leviticus 17:13)
207. Not to take the mother bird from her children (Deuteronomy 22:6)
208. To release the mother bird if she was taken from the nest (Deuteronomy 22:7)
209. Not to swear falsely in God's name (Leviticus 19:12)
210. Not to take God's name in vain (Exodus 20:6)
211. Not to deny possession of something entrusted to you (Leviticus 19:11)
212. Not to swear in denial of a monetary claim (Leviticus 19:11)
213. To swear in God's name to confirm the truth when deemed necessary by court (Deuteronomy 10:20)
214. To fulfill what was uttered and to do what was avowed (Deuteronomy 23:24)
215. Not to break oaths or vows (Numbers 30:3)
216. For oaths and vows annulled, there are the laws of annulling vows explicit in the Torah (Numbers 30:3)
217. The Nazir must let his hair grow (Numbers 6:5)
218. He must not cut his hair (Numbers 6:5)
219. He must not drink wine, wine mixtures, or wine vinegar (Numbers 6:3)
220. He must not eat fresh grapes (Numbers 6:3)
221. He must not eat raisins (Numbers 6:3)
222. He must not eat grape seeds (Numbers 6:4)
223. He must not eat grape skins (Numbers 6:4)
224. He must not be under the same roof as a corpse (Numbers 6:6)
225. He must not come into contact with the dead (Numbers 6:7)

226. He must shave after bringing sacrifices upon completion of his Nazirite period (Numbers 6:9)
227. To estimate the value of people as determined by the Torah (Leviticus 27:2)
228. To estimate the value of consecrated animals (Leviticus 27:12-13)
229. To estimate the value of consecrated houses (Leviticus 27:14)
230. To estimate the value of consecrated fields (Leviticus 27:16)
231. Carry out the laws of interdicting possessions (cherem) (Leviticus 27:28)
232. Not to sell the cherem (Leviticus 27:28)
233. Not to redeem the cherem (Leviticus 27:28)
234. Not to plant diverse seeds together (Leviticus 19:19)
235. Not to plant grains or greens in a vineyard (Deuteronomy 22:9)
236. Not to crossbreed animals (Leviticus 19:19)
237. Not to work different animals together (Deuteronomy 22:10)
238. Not to wear shatnez, a cloth woven of wool and linen (Deuteronomy 22:11)
239. To leave a corner of the field uncut for the poor (Leviticus 19:10)
240. Not to reap that corner (Leviticus 19:9)
241. To leave gleanings (Leviticus 19:9)
242. Not to gather the gleanings (Leviticus 19:9)
243. To leave the gleanings of a vineyard (Leviticus 19:10)
244. Not to gather the gleanings of a vineyard (Leviticus 19:10)
245. To leave the unformed clusters of grapes (Leviticus 19:10)
246. Not to pick the unformed clusters of grapes (Leviticus 19:10)
247. To leave the forgotten sheaves in the field (Deuteronomy 24:19)
248. Not to retrieve them (Deuteronomy 24:19)
249. To separate the tithe for the poor (Deuteronomy 14:28)
250. To give charity (Deuteronomy 15:8)
251. Not to withhold charity from the poor (Deuteronomy 15:7)
252. To set aside Terumah Gedolah (tithe for the Kohen) (Deuteronomy 18:4)
253. The Levite must set aside a tenth of his tithe (Numbers 18:26)
254. Not to preface one tithe to the next, but separate them in their proper order (Exodus 22:28)
255. A non-Kohen must not eat Terumah (Leviticus 22:10)

256. A hired worker or a Jewish bondsman of a Kohen must not eat Terumah (Leviticus 22:10)

257. An uncircumcised Kohen must not eat Terumah (Exodus 12:48)

258. An impure Kohen must not eat Terumah (Leviticus 22:4)

259. A chalalah must not eat Terumah (Leviticus 22:12)

260. To set aside Ma'aser (tithe) each planting year and give it to a Levite (Numbers 18:24)

261. To set aside the second tithe (Ma'aser Sheni) (Deuteronomy 14:22)

262. Not to spend its redemption money on anything but food, drink, or ointment (Deuteronomy 26:14)

263. Not to eat Ma'aser Sheni while impure (Deuteronomy 26:14)

264. A mourner on the first day after death must not eat Ma'aser Sheni (Deuteronomy 26:14)

265. Not to eat Ma'aser Sheni grains outside Jerusalem (Deuteronomy 12:17)

266. Not to eat Ma'aser Sheni wine products outside Jerusalem (Deuteronomy 12:17)

267. Not to eat Ma'aser Sheni oil outside Jerusalem (Deuteronomy 12:17)

268. The *fourth* year crops must be totally for holy purposes like Ma'aser Sheni (Leviticus 19:24)

269. To read the confession of tithes every *fourth* and *seventh* year (Deuteronomy 26:13)

270. To set aside the first fruits and bring them to the Temple (Exodus 23:19)

271. The Kohanim must not eat the first fruits outside Jerusalem (Deuteronomy 12:17

272. To read the Torah portion pertaining to their presentation (Deuteronomy 26:5)

273. To set aside a portion of dough for a Kohen (Numbers 15:20)

274. To give the shoulder, two cheeks, and stomach of slaughtered animals to a Kohen (Deuteronomy 18:3)

275. To give the first sheering of sheep to a Kohen (Deuteronomy 18:4)

276. To redeem the firstborn sons and give the money to a Kohen (Numbers 18:15)

277. To redeem the firstborn donkey by giving a lamb to a Kohen (Exodus 13:13)

278. To break the neck of the donkey if the owner does not intend to redeem it (Exodus 13:13)
279. To rest the land during the *seventh* year by not doing any work which enhances growth (Exodus 34:21
280. Not to work the land during the *seventh* year (Leviticus 25:4)
281. Not to work with trees to produce fruit during that year (Leviticus 25:4)
282. Not to reap crops that grow wild that year in the normal manner (Leviticus 25:5)
283. Not to gather grapes which grow wild that year in the normal way (Leviticus 25:5)
284. To leave free all produce which grew in that year (Exodus 23:11)
285. To release all loans during the *seventh* year (Deuteronomy 15:2)
286. Not to pressure or claim from the borrower (Deuteronomy 15:2)
287. Not to refrain from lending immediately before the release of the loans for fear of monetary loss (Deuteronomy 15:9)
288. The Sanhedrin must count *seven* groups of *seven* years (Leviticus 25:8)
289. The Sanhedrin must sanctify the fiftieth year (Leviticus 25:10)
290. To blow the Shofar on the tenth of Tishrei to free the slaves (Leviticus 25:9)
291. Not to work the soil during the fiftieth year (Jubilee) (Leviticus 25:11)
292. Not to reap in the normal manner that which grows wild in the fiftieth year (Leviticus 25:11)
293. Not to pick grapes which grew wild in the normal manner in the fiftieth year (Leviticus 25:11)
294. Carry out the laws of sold family properties (Leviticus 25:24)
295. Not to sell the land in Israel indefinitely (Leviticus 25:23)
296. Carry out the laws of houses in walled cities (Leviticus 25:29)
297. Tribe of Levi must not be given a portion of the land in Israel, rather they are given cities to dwell in (Deuteronomy 18:1)
298. The Levites must not take a share in the spoils of war (Deuteronomy 18:1)
299. To give the Levites cities to inhabit and their surrounding fields (Numbers 35:2)

300. Not to sell the fields but they shall remain the Levites' before and after the Jubilee year (Leviticus 25:34)
301. To build a Sanctuary (Exodus 25:8)
302. Not to build the altar with stones hewn by metal (Exodus 20:23)
303. Not to climb steps to the altar (Exodus 20:26)
304. To show reverence to the Temple (Leviticus 19:30)
305. To guard the Temple area (Numbers 18:2)
306. Not to leave the Temple unguarded (Numbers 18:5)
307. To prepare the anointing oil (Exodus 30:31)
308. Not to reproduce the anointing oil (Exodus 30:32)
309. Not to anoint with anointing oil (Exodus 30:32)
310. Not to reproduce the incense formula (Exodus 30:37)
311. Not to burn anything on the Golden Altar besides incense (Exodus 30:9)
312. The Levites must transport the ark on their shoulders (Numbers 7:9)
313. Not to remove the staves from the ark (Exodus 25:15)
314. The Levites must work in the Temple (Numbers 18:23)
315. No Levite must do another's work of either a Kohen or a Levite (Numbers 18:3)
316. To dedicate the Kohen for service (Leviticus 21:8)
317. The work of the Kohanim 's shifts must be equal during holidays (Deuteronomy 18:6-8)
318. The Kohanim must wear their priestly garments during service (Exodus 28:2)
319. Not to tear the priestly garments (Exodus 28:32)
320. The Kohen Gadol 's breastplate must not be loosened from the Efod (Exodus 28:28)
321. A Kohen must not enter the Temple intoxicated (Leviticus 10:9)
322. A Kohen must not enter the Temple with long hair (Leviticus 10:6)
323. A Kohen must not enter the Temple with torn clothes (Leviticus 10:6)
324. A Kohen must not enter the Temple indiscriminately (Leviticus 16:2)
325. A Kohen must not leave the Temple during service (Leviticus 10:7
326. To send the impure from the Temple (Numbers 5:2)
327. Impure people must not enter the Temple (Numbers 5:3)
328. Impure people must not enter the Temple Mount area (Deuteronomy 23:11)

329. Impure Kohanim must not do service in the temple (Leviticus 22:2)

330. An impure Kohen, following immersion, must wait until after sundown before returning to service (Leviticus 22:7)

331. A Kohen must wash his hands and feet before service (Exodus 30:19)

332. A Kohen with a physical blemish must not enter the sanctuary or approach the altar (Leviticus 21:23)

333. A Kohen with a physical blemish must not serve (Leviticus 21:17)

334. A Kohen with a temporary blemish must not serve (Leviticus 21:17)

335. One who is not a Kohen must not serve (Numbers 18:4)

336. To offer only unblemished animals (Leviticus 22:21)

337. Not to dedicate a blemished animal for the altar (Leviticus 22:20)

338. Not to slaughter it (Leviticus 22:22)

339. Not to sprinkle its blood (Leviticus 22:24)

340. Not to burn its fat (Leviticus 22:22)

341. Not to offer a temporarily blemished animal (Deuteronomy 17:1)

342. Not to sacrifice blemished animals even if offered by non-Jews (Leviticus 22:25)

343. Not to inflict wounds upon dedicated animals (Leviticus 22:21)

344. To redeem dedicated animals which have become disqualified (Deuteronomy 12:15)

345. To offer only animals which are at least *eight* days old (Leviticus 22:27)

345. Not to offer animals bought with the wages of a harlot or the animal exchanged for a dog (Deuteronomy 23:19)

347. Not to burn honey or yeast on the altar (Leviticus 2:11)

348. To salt all sacrifices (Leviticus 2:13)

349. Not to omit the salt from sacrifices (Leviticus 2:13)

350. Carry out the procedure of the burnt offering as prescribed in the Torah (Leviticus 1:3)

351. Not to eat its meat (Deuteronomy 12:17)

352. Carry out the procedure of the sin offering (Leviticus 6:18)

353. Not to eat the meat of the inner sin offering (Leviticus 6:23)

354. Not to decapitate a fowl brought as a sin offering (Leviticus 5:8)

355. Carry out the procedure of the guilt offering (Leviticus 7:1)

356. The Kohanim must eat the sacrificial meat in the Temple (Exodus 29:33)

357. The Kohanim must not eat the meat outside the Temple courtyard (Deuteronomy 12:17)

358. A non-Kohen must not eat sacrificial meat (Exodus 29:33)
359. To follow the procedure of the peace offering (Leviticus 7:11)
360. Not to eat the meat of minor sacrifices before sprinkling the blood (Deuteronomy 12:17)
361. To bring meal offerings as prescribed in the Torah (Leviticus 2:1)
362. Not to put oil on the meal offerings of wrongdoers (Leviticus 5:11)
363. Not to put frankincense on the meal offerings of wrongdoers (Leviticus 3:11)
364. Not to eat the meal offering of the High Priest (Leviticus 6:16)
365. Not to bake a meal offering as leavened bread (Leviticus 6:10)
366. The Kohanim must eat the remains of the meal offerings (Leviticus 6:9)
367. To bring all avowed and freewill offerings to the Temple on the first subsequent festival (Deuteronomy 12:5-6)
368. Not to withhold payment incurred by any vow (Deuteronomy 23:22)
369. To offer all sacrifices in the Temple (Deuteronomy 12:11)
370. To bring all sacrifices from outside Israel to the Temple (Deuteronomy 12:26)
371. Not to slaughter sacrifices outside the courtyard (Leviticus 17:4)
372. Not to offer any sacrifices outside the courtyard (Deuteronomy 12:13)
373. To offer *two* lambs every day (Numbers 28:3)
374. To light a fire on the altar every day (Leviticus 6:6)
375. Not to extinguish this fire (Leviticus 6:6)
376. To remove the ashes from the altar every day (Leviticus 6:3)
377. To burn incense every day (Exodus 30:7)
378. To light the Menorah every day (Exodus 27:21)
379. The Kohen Gadol (High Priest) must bring a meal offering every day (Leviticus 6:13)
380. To bring *two* additional lambs as burnt offerings on Shabbat (Numbers 28:3)
381. To make the show bread (Exodus 25:30)
382. To bring additional offerings on Rosh Chodesh (The New Month) (Numbers 28:11)
383. To bring additional offerings on Passover (Numbers 28:19)
384. To offer the wave offering from the meal of the new wheat (Leviticus 23:10)

385. Each man must count the Omer—*seven* weeks from the day the new wheat offering was brought (Leviticus 23:15)
386. To bring additional offerings on Shavuot (Numbers 28:26)
387. To bring *two* leaves to accompany the above sacrifice (Leviticus 23:17)
388. To bring additional offerings on Rosh Hashana (Numbers 29:2)
389. To bring additional offerings on Yom Kippur (Numbers 29:8)
390. To bring additional offerings on Sukkot (Numbers 29:13)
391. To bring additional offerings on Shmini Atzeret (Numbers 29:35)
392. Not to eat sacrifices which have become unfit or blemished (Deuteronomy 14.3)
393. Not to eat from sacrifices offered with improper intentions (Leviticus 7:18)
394. Not to leave sacrifices past the time allowed for eating them (Leviticus 22:30)
395. Not to eat from that which was left over (Leviticus 19:8)
396. Not to eat from sacrifices which became impure (Leviticus 7:19)
397. An impure person must not eat from sacrifices (Leviticus 7:20)
398. To burn the leftover sacrifices (Leviticus 7:17)
399. To burn all impure sacrifices (Leviticus 7:19)
400. To follow the procedure of Yom Kippur in the sequence prescribed in Parshah Acharei Mot (after the death of Aaron's sons …) (Leviticus 16:3)
401. One who profaned property must repay what he profaned plus a fifth and bring a sacrifice (Leviticus 5:16)
402. Not to work consecrated animals (Deuteronomy 15:19)
403. Not to shear the fleece of consecrated animals (Deuteronomy 15:19)
403. To slaughter the paschal sacrifice at the specified time (Exodus 12:6)
405. Not to slaughter it while in possession of leaven (Exodus 23:18)
406. Not to leave the fat overnight (Exodus 23:18)
407. To slaughter the second Paschal Lamb (Numbers 9:11)
408. To eat the Paschal Lamb with matzah and Marror on the night of the fourteenth of Nissan (Exodus 12:8)
409. To eat the second Paschal Lamb on the night of the 15th of Iyar (Numbers 9:11)
410. Not to eat the paschal meat raw or boiled (Exodus 12:9)

411. Not to take the paschal meat from the confines of the group (Exodus 12:46)
412. An apostate must not eat from it (Exodus 12:43)
413. A permanent or temporary hired worker must not eat from it (Exodus 12:45)
414. An uncircumcised male must not eat from it (Exodus 12:48)
415. Not to break any bones from the paschal offering (Exodus 12:46)
416. Not to break any bones from the second paschal offering (Numbers 9:12)
417. Not to leave any meat from the paschal offering over until morning (Exodus 12:10)
418. Not to leave the second paschal meat over until morning (Numbers 9:12)
419. Not to leave the meat of the holiday offering of the 14th until the 16th (Deuteronomy 16:4)
420. To be seen at the Temple on Passover, Shavuot, and Sukkot (Deuteronomy 16:16)
421. To celebrate on these *three* festivals (bring a peace offering) (Exodus 23:14)
422. To rejoice on these *three* festivals (bring a peace offering) (Deuteronomy 16:14)
423. Not to appear at the Temple without offerings (Deuteronomy 16:16)
424. Not to refrain from rejoicing with, and giving gifts to, the Levites (Deuteronomy 12:19)
425. To assemble all the people on the Sukkot following the *seventh* year (Deuteronomy 31:12)
426. To set aside the firstborn animals (Exodus 13:12)
427. The Kohanim must not eat unblemished firstborn animals outside Jerusalem (Deuteronomy 12:17)
428. Not to redeem the firstborn (Numbers 18:17)
429. Separate the tithe from animals (Leviticus 27:32)
430. Not to redeem the tithe (Leviticus 27:33)
431. Every person must bring a sin offering (in the temple) for his transgression (Leviticus 4:27)
432. Bring an asham talui (temple offering) when uncertain of guilt (Leviticus 5:17-18)

433. Bring an asham vadai (temple offering) when guilt is ascertained (Leviticus 5:25)
434. Bring an oleh v'yored (temple offering) offering (if the person is wealthy, an animal; if poor, a bird or meal offering) (Leviticus 5:7-11)
435. The Sanhedrin must bring an offering (in the Temple) when it rules in error (Leviticus 4:13)
436. A woman who had a running (vaginal) issue must bring an offering (in the Temple) after she goes to the Mikveh (Leviticus 15:28-29)
437. A woman who gave birth must bring an offering (in the Temple) after she goes to the Mikveh (Leviticus 12:6)
438. A man who had a running (unnatural urinary) issue must bring an offering (in the Temple) after he goes to the Mikveh (Leviticus 15:13-14)
439. A metzora must bring an offering (in the Temple) after going to the Mikveh (Leviticus 14:10)
440. Not to substitute another beast for one set apart for sacrifice (Leviticus 27:10)
441. The new animal, in addition to the substituted one, retains consecration (Leviticus 27:10)
442. Not to change consecrated animals from one type of offering to another (Leviticus 27:26)
443. Carry out the laws of impurity of the dead (Numbers 19:14)
444. Carry out the procedure of the Red Heifer (Para Aduma) (Numbers 19:2)
445. Carry out the laws of the sprinkling water (Numbers 19:21)
446. Rule the laws of human tzara'at as prescribed in the Torah (Leviticus 13:12)
447. The metzora must not remove his signs of impurity (Deuteronomy 24:8)
448. The metzora must not shave signs of impurity in his hair (Leviticus 13:33)
449. The metzora must publicize his condition by tearing his garments, allowing his hair to grow and covering his lips (Leviticus 13:45)
450. Carry out the prescribed rules for purifying the metzora (Leviticus 14:2)
451. The metzora must shave off all his hair prior to purification (Leviticus 14:9)

452. Carry out the laws of tzara'at of clothing (Leviticus 13:47)
453. Carry out the laws of tzara'at of houses (Leviticus 13:34)
454. Observe the laws of menstrual impurity (Leviticus 15:19)
455. Observe the laws of impurity caused by childbirth (Leviticus 12:2)
456. Observe the laws of impurity caused by a woman's running issue (Leviticus 15:25)
457. Observe the laws of impurity caused by a man's running issue (irregular ejaculation of infected semen) (Leviticus 15:3)
458. Observe the laws of impurity caused by a dead beast (Leviticus 11:39)
459. Observe the laws of impurity caused by the *eight* shratzim (insects) (Leviticus 11:29)
460. Observe the laws of impurity of a seminal emission (regular ejaculation, with normal semen) (Leviticus 15:16)
461. Observe the laws of impurity concerning liquid and solid foods (Leviticus 11:34)
462. Every impure person must immerse himself in a Mikveh to become pure (Leviticus 15:16)
463. The court must judge the damages incurred by a goring ox (Exodus 21:28)
464. The court must judge the damages incurred by an animal eating (Exodus 22:4)
465. The court must judge the damages incurred by a pit (Exodus 21:33)
466. The court must judge the damages incurred by fire (Exodus 22:5)
467. Not to steal money stealthily (Leviticus 19:11)
468. The court must implement punitive measures against the thief (Exodus 21:37)
469. Each individual must ensure that his scales and weights are accurate (Leviticus 19:36)
470. Not to commit injustice with scales and weights (Leviticus 19:35)
471. Not to possess inaccurate scales and weights even if they are not for use (Deuteronomy 25:13)
472. Not to move a boundary marker to steal someone's property (Deuteronomy 19:14)
473. Not to kidnap (Exodus 20:13)
474. Not to rob openly (Leviticus 19:13)
475. Not to withhold wages or fail to repay a debt (Leviticus 19:13)

476. Not to covet and scheme to acquire another's possession (Exodus 20:14)
477. Not to desire another's possession (Deuteronomy 5:18)
478. Return the robbed object or its value (Leviticus 5:23)
479. Not to ignore a lost object (Deuteronomy 22:3)
480. Return the lost object (Deuteronomy 22:1)
481. The court must implement laws against the one who assaults another or damages another's property (Exodus 21:18)
482. Not to murder (Exodus 20:13)
483. Not to accept monetary restitution to atone for the murderer (Numbers 35:31)
484. The court must send the accidental murderer to a city of refuge (Numbers 35:25)
485. Not to accept monetary restitution instead of being sent to a city of refuge (Numbers 35:32)
486. Not to kill the murderer before he stands trial (Numbers 35:12)
487. Save someone being pursued even by taking the life of the pursuer (Deuteronomy 25:12)
488. Not to pity the pursuer (Numbers 35:12)
489. Not to stand idly by if someone's life is in danger (Leviticus 19:16)
490. Designate cities of refuge and prepare routes of access (Deuteronomy 19:3)
491. Break the neck of a calf by the river valley following an unsolved murder (Deuteronomy 21:4)
492. Not to work nor plant that river valley (Deuteronomy 21:4)
493. Not to allow pitfalls and obstacles to remain on your property (Deuteronomy 22:8)
494. Make a guard rail around flat roofs (Deuteronomy 22:8)
495. Not to put a stumbling block before a blind man (nor give harmful advice) (Lifnei iver) (Leviticus 19:14)
496. Help another remove the load from a beast which can no longer carry it (Exodus 23:5)
497. Help others load their beast (Deuteronomy 22:4)
498. Not to leave others distraught with their burdens (but to help either load or unload) (Deuteronomy 22:4)
499. Buy and sell according to Torah law (Leviticus 25:14)
500. Not to overcharge or underpay for an article (Leviticus 25:14)

501. Not to insult or harm anybody with words (Leviticus 25:17)
502. Not to cheat a sincere convert monetarily (Exodus 22:20)
503. Not to insult or harm a sincere convert with words (Exodus 22:20)
504. Purchase a Hebrew slave in accordance with the prescribed laws (Exodus 21:2)
505. Not to sell him as a slave is sold (Leviticus 25:42)
506. Not to work him oppressively (Leviticus 25:43)
507. Not to allow a non-Jew to work him oppressively (Leviticus 25:53)
508. Not to have him do menial slave labor (Leviticus 25:39)
509. Give him gifts when he goes free (Deuteronomy 15:14)
510. Not to send him away empty-handed (Deuteronomy 15:13)
511. Redeem Jewish maidservants (Exodus 21:8)
512. Betroth the Jewish maidservant (Exodus 21:8)
513. The master must not sell his maidservant (Exodus 21:8)
514. Canaanite slaves must work forever unless injured in one of their limbs (Leviticus 25:46)
515. Not to extradite a slave who fled to (biblical) Israel (Deuteronomy 23:16)
516. Not to wrong a slave who has come to Israel for refuge (Deuteronomy 23:16)
517. The courts must carry out the laws of a hired worker and hired guard (Exodus 22:9)
518. Pay wages on the day they were earned (Deuteronomy 24:15)
519. Not to delay payment of wages past the agreed time (Leviticus 19:13)
520. The hired worker may eat from the unharvested crops where he works (Deuteronomy 23:25)
521. The worker must not eat while on hired time (Deuteronomy 23:26)
522. The worker must not take more than he can eat (Deuteronomy 23:25)
523. Not to muzzle an ox while plowing (Deuteronomy 25:4)
524. The courts must carry out the laws of a borrower (Exodus 22:13)
525. The courts must carry out the laws of an unpaid guard (Exodus 22:6)
526. Lend to the poor and destitute (Exodus 22:24)
527. To press them for payment if you know they don't have it (Exodus 22:24)
528. Press the idolater for payment (Deuteronomy 15:3)
529. The creditor must not forcibly take collateral (Deuteronomy 24:10)
530. Return the collateral to the debtor when needed (Deuteronomy 24:13)

531. Not to delay its return when needed (Deuteronomy 24:12)
532. Not to demand collateral from a widow (Deuteronomy 24:17)
533. Not to demand as collateral utensils needed for preparing food (Deuteronomy 24:6)
534. Not to lend with interest (Leviticus 25:37)
535. Not to borrow with interest (Deuteronomy 23:20)
536. Not to intermediate in an interest loan, guarantee, witness, or write the promissory note (Exodus 22:24)
537. Lend to and borrow from idolaters with interest (Deuteronomy 23:21)
538. The courts must carry out the laws of the plaintiff, admitter, or denier (Exodus 22:8)
539. Carry out the laws of the order of inheritance (Numbers 27:8)
540. Appoint judges (Deuteronomy 16:18)
541. Not to appoint judges who are not familiar with judicial procedure (Deuteronomy 1:17)
542. Decide by majority in case of disagreement (Exodus 23:2)
543. The court must not execute through a majority of one; at least a majority of two is required (Exodus 23:2)
544. A judge who presented an acquittal plea must not present an argument for conviction in capital cases (Deuteronomy 23:2)
545. The courts must carry out the death penalty of stoning (Deuteronomy 22:24)
546. The courts must carry out the death penalty of burning (Leviticus 20:14)
547. The courts must carry out the death penalty of the sword (Exodus 21:20)
548. The courts must carry out the death penalty of strangulation (Leviticus 20:10)
549. The courts must hang those stoned for blasphemy or idolatry (Deuteronomy 21:22)
550. Bury the executed on the day they are killed (Deuteronomy 21:23)
551. Not to delay burial overnight (Deuteronomy 21:23)
552. The court must not let the sorcerer live (Exodus 22:17)
553. The court must give lashes to the wrongdoer (Exodus 25:2)
554. The court must not exceed the prescribed number of lashes (Deuteronomy 25:3)

555. The court must not kill anybody on circumstantial evidence (Exodus 23:7)
556. The court must not punish anybody who was forced to do a crime (Deuteronomy 22:26)
557. A judge must not pity the murderer or assaulter at the trial (Deuteronomy 19:13)
558. A judge must not have mercy on the poor man at the trial (Leviticus 19:15)
559. A judge must not respect the great man at the trial (Leviticus 19:15)
560. A judge must not decide unjustly the case of the habitual transgressor (Exodus 23:6)
561. A judge must not pervert justice (Leviticus 19:15)
562. A judge must not pervert a case involving a convert or orphan (Deuteronomy 24:17)
563. Judge righteously (Leviticus 19:15)
564. The judge must not fear a violent man in judgment (Deuteronomy 1:17)
565. Judges must not accept bribes (Exodus 23:8)
566. Judges must not accept testimony unless both parties are present (Exodus 23:1)
567. Not to curse judges (Exodus 22:27)
568. Not to curse the head of state or leader of the Sanhedrin (Exodus 22:27)
569. Not to curse any upstanding Jew (Leviticus 19:14)
570. Anybody who knows evidence must testify in court (Leviticus 5:1)
571. Carefully interrogate the witness (Deuteronomy 13:15)
572. A witness must not serve as a judge in capital crimes (Deuteronomy 19:17)
573. Not to accept testimony from a lone witness (Deuteronomy 19:15)
574. Transgressors must not testify (Exodus 23:1)
575. Relatives of the litigants must not testify (Deuteronomy 24:16)
576. Not to testify falsely (Exodus 20:13)
577. Punish the false witnesses as they tried to punish the defendant (Deuteronomy 19:19)
578. Act according to the ruling of the Sanhedrin (Deuteronomy 17:11)
579. Not to deviate from the word of the Sanhedrin (Deuteronomy 17:11)

580. Not to add to the Torah commandments or their oral explanations (Deuteronomy 13:1)
581. Not to diminish from the Torah any commandments, in whole or in part (Deuteronomy 13:1)
582. Not to curse your father and mother (Exodus 21:17)
583. Not to strike your father and mother (Exodus 21:15)
584. Respect your father or mother (Exodus 20:12)
585. Fear your father or mother (Leviticus 19:3)
586. Not to be a rebellious son (Deuteronomy 21:18)
587. Mourn for relatives (Leviticus 10:19)
588. The High Priest must not defile himself for any relative (Leviticus 21:11)
589. The High Priest must not enter under the same roof as a corpse (Leviticus 21:11)
590. A Kohen must not defile himself (by going to funerals or cemeteries) for anyone except relatives (Leviticus 21:1)
591. Appoint a king from Israel (Deuteronomy 17:15)
592. Not to appoint a convert (Deuteronomy 17:15)
593. The king must not have too many wives (Deuteronomy 17:17)
594. The king must not have too many horses (Deuteronomy 17:16)
595. The king must not have too much silver and gold (Deuteronomy 17:17)
596. Destroy the *seven* Canaanite nations (Deuteronomy 20:17)
597. Not to let any of them remain alive (Deuteronomy 20:16)
598. Wipe out the descendants of Amalek (Deuteronomy 25:19)
599. Remember what Amalek did to the Jewish people (Deuteronomy 25:17)
600. Not to forget Amalek's atrocities and ambush on our journey from Egypt in the desert (Deuteronomy 25:19)
601. Not to dwell permanently in Egypt (Deuteronomy 17:16)
602. Offer peace terms to the inhabitants of a city while holding siege, and treat them according to the Torah if they accept the terms (Deuteronomy 20:10)
603. Not to offer peace to Ammon and Moab while besieging them (Deuteronomy 23:7)
604. Not to destroy fruit trees even during the siege (Deuteronomy 20:19)
605. Prepare latrines outside the camps (Deuteronomy 23:13)

606. Prepare a shovel for each soldier to dig with (Deuteronomy 23:14)
607. Appoint a priest to speak with the soldiers during the war (Deuteronomy 20:2)
608. He who has taken a wife, built a new home, or planted a vineyard is given a year to rejoice with his possessions (Deuteronomy 24:5)
609. Not to demand from the above any involvement, communal or military (Deuteronomy 24:5)
610. Not to panic and retreat during battle (Deuteronomy 20:3)
611. Keep the laws of the captive woman (Deuteronomy 21:11)
612. Not to sell her into slavery (Deuteronomy 21:14)
613. Not to retain her for servitude after having sexual relations with her (Deuteronomy 21:14)

Appendix C

What about the Apocrypha?

The current books of the Bible were not always together as they are today. The 39 (3 + 9 = 12, 1 + 2 = 3) books of the Old Testament have probably been together in one collection since over 300 years before Christ, although their order has changed. Other books considered as secondary, but still revered, have been included off and on with the Old Testament until present day. The 27 (2 + 7 = 9) books of the New Testament did not come together until over 350 years after Christ's death, although most of them were accepted very early. Many other gospels and histories based around Jesus and/or his disciples were written but not included in the New Testament.

Who made the decisions on what books to include and which books to discard? Various religious councils have met over the centuries to test books for inclusion. Why did they discard some books that had been known and read for centuries? They were unsure of the validity or authority of the author, the geographical source, or the content—or they did not agree that the message contained in the book was consistent with the message found in the rest of the Bible. Why did these religious councils have to be so careful, and why was their task not obvious? There were scores of books from which to choose. Though some of these books are lost today, many of them are still available in print. With any great person or time, there is a need in the people of that time or the time to follow, to embellish the actual historical fact with legends or tall tales. Even now there are legends concerning people such as George Washington or Davy Crockett. It has been this way throughout history: read the biographies of such people as Alexander the Great or Julius Caesar. One of the most difficult challenges historians have is sorting fact from fiction. Given the greatness of the prophets of the Old

Testament or of Jesus and his disciples in the New Testament, it is no wonder the same kinds of stories were written concerning them.

The term *apocryphal* means hidden or secret, of uncertain authorship and/or authenticity. The Apocrypha is the name given to books that some argue should be part of the Jewish and/or Christian canons—those books considered official by the church. There are up to 100 such books, more than the combined Old and New Testaments as they exist today. With all this debate, it is no wonder different versions of the Bible exist, composed of different sets of books. For example, 11 apocryphal books are included in the Roman Catholic Douay Bible that are not in the Protestant Bible. Most of these books were written in the last three centuries before Christ—after the time of Old Testament prophecy. They are partly historical, connecting the time of the Old Testament and the time of the New Testament. They are partly allegorical—stories that on the surface seem simple but are really portraying a much deeper message. Several of these 11 books have periodically been considered more valid for inclusion than some of the disputed books of the New Testament.

Why include this discussion in a book on the numbers of the Bible? Given that you know the numbers in the Bible follow a divine numeric code, and given that you understand the keys to that code, you should be able to improve the quality of your judgment in considering the validity of apocryphal books for inclusion in the Word of God. I will not attempt to reach that conclusion in these pages. The few examples of the numeric code included in this chapter are not enough to come to a dependable conclusion about the books quoted. It will be up to you to make up your mind through additional reading and study of the Apocrypha.

Numbers in the Apocrypha

I have organized the following examples in order by number. Beside each number will be a reminder of the meaning of that number.

One—Pertaining to God

There is *one* wise and greatly to be feared, the Lord sitting upon his throne. (Ecclesiasticus 1:8)

Now therefore let us cry unto heaven, if peradventure the Lord will have mercy upon us, and remember the covenants of our fathers, and destroy this host before our face this day: That so all the heathen may know that there is *one* who delivereth and saveth Israel. (1 Maccabees 4:10-11)

Two—Pairs of Opposites

Woe be to fearful hearts, and faint hearts, and the sinner that goeth *two* ways! (Ecclesiasticus 2:12)

Three—The Holy Trinity

Then *three* young men, that were of the guard that kept the king's body, spake one to another; Let everyone of us speak a sentence: he that shall overcome, and whose sentence shall seem wiser than the others, unto him shall the king Darius give great gifts, and great things in token of victory. (1 Esdras 3:4-5)

Four—Physical World

And bowing the heavens, Thou didst set fast the earth, movedst the whole world, and madest the depths to tremble, and troublest the men of that age. And that glory went through *four* gates, of fire, and of earthquake, and of wind, and of cold; that Thou mightest give the law unto the seed of Jacob, and diligence unto the generation of Israel. (2 Esdras 3:18-19)

For in the long garment was the whole world, and in the *four* rows of the stones was the glory of the fathers graven, and Thy Majesty upon the diadem of his head. (Wisdom of Solomon 18:24)

Five—Physical Body

And the cisterns were emptied, and they had not water to drink their fill for one day; for they gave them drink by measure. Therefore the young children were out of heart, and their women and young men fainted for thirst, and fell down in the streets of the city, and by the passages of the gates, and there was no longer any strength in them.... Then said Ozias to them, Brethren, be of good courage, let us yet endure *five* days, in which space the Lord our God may turn His mercy toward us; for He will not forsake us utterly. (Judith 7:21-22, 30)

Six—Man

Now when the king saw that they pressed him sore, being constrained, he delivered Daniel unto them: Who cast him into the lion's den: where he was *six* days. (Bel and the Dragon 30-31)

Seven—Perfection

I am Raphael, one of the *seven* holy angels, which present the prayers of the saints, and which go in and out before the glory of the Holy *One*. (Tobit 12:15)

Give unto the most High according as He hath enriched thee; and as thou hast gotten, give with a cheerful eye. For the Lord recompenseth, and will give thee *seven* times as much. (Ecclesiasticus 35:10-11)

Eight—Completed Evolution

So Tobit made an end of praising God. And he was eight and fifty years old when he lost his sight, which was restored to him after *eight* years: and he gave alms, and he increased in the fear of the Lord God, and praised him. (Tobit 14:1-2)

Nine—The Ending

For Thou art alone, and we all *one* workmanship of Thine hands, like as Thou hast said. For when the body is fashioned now in the mother's womb, and Thou givest it members, Thy creature is preserved in fire and water, and *nine* months doth thy workmanship endure thy creature which is created within her. (2 Esdras 8:7-8)

Summary

Throughout history, religious scholars have debated whether various apocryphal books should be included or excluded from the Bible. Knowing the keys to the numeric code used in the Bible is an aide for each of you to make your own judgment as to whether an apocryphal book should be included. Though by itself the numeric code may not allow you to make an authoritative ruling, knowing the code makes reading an already interesting set of books even more rewarding.

Appendix D

Alternative Gematria and Isopsephy Methodologies

Overview

As discussed previously, there is a large field of study around the conversion of letters, names, words, and phrases to their numerical equivalents. When this science involves Hebrew, it is called *gematria*, and when it involves Greek, it is called *isopsephy*. One belief is that since God created the universe via the spoken word, each letter carries with it a different inherent force or energy. When the letters are combined into words or phrases, their essences combine as well to create new meaning. When multiple words and phrases have the same total, it is not a coincidence but instead an indication of an interrelationship that may not be obvious from the strict denotation of the word.

In the text of this book I have presented an analysis using the *standard reduced* methodology. That is, I assigned the numeric equivalent to each letter in the word or phrase and then added the numeric values to find the total value of the word or phrase. This approach is the standard methodology. Continuing to add the individual digits until the number is converted to a single digit is called the reduced methodology. By combining the two practices, I was following the standard reduced methodology.

Other methodologies in this field of study include the following:

- Sofit value
- Modified reduced value
- Full value
- Ordinal value
- Other related practices

Sofit Value

As indicated in the first chapter, the Hebrew numbering system at the time the Bible was written did not have individual numbers greater than 400. Later, larger numbers up to 900 were added using the variant forms of some letters that were written differently if they were the last letter (Sof) in the word. In the standard methodology, the final form of a letter carries the same numerical value as the letter when it appears within a word. Sofit value refers to the numerical value of a word when the higher value is used for a final form letter.

For example, the word *shalom* is written with the letters Shin, Lamed, Vav, and Mem-F. The standard value of Mem is 40. The value of the variant form, Mem-F, is 600. Therefore the standard value of shalom is different from the sofit value:

Shalom

שלום

$$\text{Standard Value} = 300 + 30 + 6 + 40 = 402$$

$$4 + 0 + 2 = 6$$

$$\text{Sofit Value} = 300 + 30 + 6 + 600 = 936$$

$$9 + 3 + 6 = 18$$

$$1 + 8 = 9$$

There are examples where using the sofit value instead of the standard value seems to enhance the symbolism. An example is the name Abraham:

Abraham

אברהם

Standard Value $=$ $1 + 2 + 200 + 5 + 40 = 248$

$$2 + 4 + 8 = 14$$

$$1 + 4 = 5$$

Sofit Value $=$ $1 + 2 + 200 + 5 + 600 = 808$

$$8 + 0 + 8 = 16$$

$$1 + 6 = 7$$

The standard value of 248 is equivalent to the standard value of the Hebrew word *rahim* which means *mercy* and has the associated symbolism that Abraham represents this attribute of God. The sofit value of 808 is equivalent to the sofit value of *the faith* as Paul writes in Romans 4:17. Some people believe this equivalent value indicates the connection between Judaism and Christianity.

Rahim (Mercy)

רחם

Standard Value $=$ $200 + 8 + 40 = 248$

$$2 + 4 + 8 = 14$$

$$1 + 4 = 5$$

He Pistis (The Faith)

η πιστις

Sofit Value $=$ $8 + 80 + 10 + 200 + 300 + 10 + 200 = 808$

$$8 + 0 + 8 = 16$$

$$1 + 6 = 7$$

Some people view the soft value as adding insight into the symbolism associated with the word. My concern with this approach stems from the knowledge that the numeric values associated with the variant forms did not exist at the time the Bible was written.

Modified Reduced Value

The standard reduced methodology reduces the value of a word or phrase to a single digit after the total value has been calculated. There is another school of thought that since there are only nine integers in the Hebrew numeric system, the value of each letter should be reduced to a single digit before adding it into the total. When the variant forms are added, there are twenty seven letters, or three sets of nine, called reduction classes. Every letter would reduce to one of nine equivalent values. In this system Dalet (*4*), Mem (40 = 4 + 0 = *4*), and Tav (400 = 4 + 0 + 0 = *4*) have the same value of *four*. Obviously, this methodology would change the implicit value and associated symbolism of a word. The resulting total value from adding the reduced values of each letter number is known as the *katan*, or small, value. Relationships of these small values and the relationships of the letters in each reduction class are thought to add more insight into the symbolic meaning of the words.

Continuing with the *shalom* example:

Shalom

שלום

Standard Value $= 300 + 30 + 6 + 40 = 402$

$$4 + 0 + 2 = 6$$

Modified Reduced or Small Value $= 3 + 3 + 6 + 4 = 16$

$$1 + 6 = 7$$

My concern with this methodology is similar to the concern I voiced for the sofit value methodology.

Full Value

As said many times, the standard value of a word is determined by adding the numeric equivalents of the letters. An alternative form for determining that value is to replace the letters with their names and then add the numeric equivalents of all the letters in those names. The resulting value is called the full value, and the word is said to be filled with the resulting value and associated symbolism.

For example, the full value of shalom is as follows:

Shalom

שלום

Standard Value $=$ $300 + 30 + 6 + 40 = 402$

$$4 + 0 + 2 = 6$$

Full Value $=$ Shin Lamed Vav Mem

$=$ $360 + 74 + 22 + 80 = 536$

$$5 + 3 + 6 = 14$$

$$1 + 4 = 5$$

One issue with full values is there are multiple possible spellings for some letters, which raises the question as to which spelling and resultant value should be used. Proponents of the full value methodology argue they are all correct. Each value represents a different aspect of the divine meaning. Because of the variant spellings of the letters Heh and Vav, the name of God, Yahweh, has a total of twenty-seven full values.

Practitioners of this approach have found many relationships of those values and other names of God discussed in Appendix A. They also have found many relationships to other key names and words. One of interest shows that the numeric value of the name Adam is the equivalent to one of the full values of the name of God, Yahweh:

> Then God said, "Let us make man in our image, in our likeness ..." (Genesis 1:26)

Adam

אדם

Standard Value   = $1 + 4 + 40 = 45$

$4 + 5 = 9$

Yahweh, or Jehovah

יהוה

Full Value   =   Yod Heh Vav Heh

$20 + 6 + 13 + 6 = 45$

$4 + 5 = 9$

Ordinal Value

Ordinal value refers to the techniques similar to modern numerology in which each of the letters in the Hebrew and/or Greek alphabet are assigned a value equivalent to their position in the alphabet. Aleph equals 1; Mem equals 13; Tav equals 22. The ordinal value can end with the last letter in the alphabet or continue with the variant letter forms. In some applications the variant forms of the letters are placed inside the alphabet next to their counterparts and assigned the appropriate ordinal value.

The word shalom then could have multiple ordinal values:

Shalom

שלום

Ordinal Value 1 = 21 + 12 + 6 + 13 = 52

5 + 2 = 7

Ordinal Value 2 = 21 + 12 + 6 + 24 = 63

6 + 3 = 9

Ordinal Value 3 = 26 + 13 + 6 + 14 = 59

5 + 9 = 14

1 + 4 = 5

I see little value in the ordinal approach because there is no tie between the letter and the numerical value assigned to the letter. There are other practices somewhat similar to the ordinal approach that may provide more significant insight. Some of those practices include:

- The placement of the word or phrase in question
  o The number of the word in the verse
  o The number of the verse in the chapter
  o The number of the chapter in the book
- The number of occurrences
  o The number of times a number appears in the Bible
  o The number of times a word appears in the Bible
  o The number of times a specific event occurs

For example, the 23rd (2 + 3 = 5) Psalm concerns God watching over our physical lives.

Conclusion

All of these alternative methodologies have many advocates, and any study of the symbolic value of Bible numbers and words will come across numerous examples that demonstrate the revelations they offer. While these methodologies can deliver very interesting results, whether they bring additional insight is up to the judgment of each individual.

Appendix E

Concordance of Numbers in the Bible

One and Equivalents

Genesis

1.9	2:21	2:24	8:5	8:19	11:1
11:6	14:13	14:20	16:3	16:13	17:17
18:32	19:17	20:3	20:16	21:5	21:15
22:2	23:1	24:2	24:10	24:14	24:22
24:44	24:60	24:63	25:23	26:10	26:12
27:38	27:45	28:11	28:22	29:26	29:27
29:33	30:31	30:42	31:7	31:8	31:41
32:17	33:13	33:19	34:15	34:16	34:22
37:20	37:36	38:28	39:1	39:11	41:25
41:26	41:38	42:6	42:11	42:13	42:16
42:19	42:27	42:33	42:38	43:29	44:2
44:16	44:20	44:28	44:29	45:4	48:18
48:22	49:16	49:24			

Exodus

2:6	2:7	2:11	2:13	6:25	9:6
9:7	11:1	12:3	12:4	12:46	12:48
14:20	14:28	16:36	17:12	20:1	20:16
21:10	22:25	24:3	25:19	25:31	25:36
26:4	26:9	26:10	27:2	27:9	27:18
28:8	28:21	30:2	34:7	34:28	36:8
36:11	36:16	36:17	37:8	37:17	37:19
37:22	38:2	38:9	38:11	38:26	38:27
39:5	39:14				

Leviticus

5:7	5:8	5:15	5:18	6:6	7:14
9:15	11:25	11:32	11:33	11:35	11:36
12:8	14:5	14:7	14:10	14:12	14:21
14:22	14:50	15:15	15:30	16:8	19:18
19:34	20:4	21:10	22:6	23:18	23:19
23:27	25:9	25:14	25:25	25:35	25:39
25:47	25:48	26:8	26:26	27:6	27:10
27:11	27:27	27:32			

Numbers

1:2	1:4	1:18	1:20	1:22	1:44
3:47	6:11	7:11	7:13	7:14	7:15
7:16	7:19	7:20	7:21	7:22	7:24
7:25	7:26	7:27	7:28	7:31	7:32
7:33	7:34	7:37	7:38	7:39	7:40
7:43	7:44	7:45	7:46	7:49	7:50
7:51	7:52	7:55	7:56	7:57	7:61
7:62	7:63	7:64	7:67	7:68	7:69
7:70	7:73	7:74	7:75	7:76	7:80
7:81	7:82	7:86	8:12	10:4	10:36
11:19	13:2	14:22	14:34	15:4	15:12
15:27	15:28	15:29	16:7	16:22	17:2
17:3	17:6	18:26	22:32	23:9	27:7
28:4	28:11	28:15	28:19	28:21	28:22
28:27	28:30	29:2	29:5	29:8	29:11
29:16	29:27	29:28	29:31	29:34	29:36
29:38	31:4	31:6	31:14	31:28	31:30
31:47	31:51	34:18	35:25		

Deuteronomy

1:11	1:16	1:23	4:13	4:34	4:42
5:1	6:4	7:9	9:3	10:4	12:14
13:12	14:22	17:2	17:6	19:5	19:11
19:15	23:2	23:3	23:10	24:5	24:9
24:11	26:12	28:7	28:55	32:22	32:30
33:17					

Joshua

3:4	3:12	4:2	4:4	10:42	15:57
15:8	17:14	17:17	20:4	21:5	22:14
22:22	23:10	24:32			

Judges

1:4	4:6	4:10	5:5	6:39	7:3
7:19	8:24	9:2	9:5	9:8	9:49
11:37	14:3	15:15	15:16	16:28	17:5
19:13	20:1	20:6	20:8	20:10	20:11
20:34	21:3	21:8	21:23		

Ruth

2:13	2:19	4:7

1 Samuel

1:8	4:6	4:10	6:7	7:3	7:19
8:15	8:17	9:3	11:7	12:13	14:36
15:1	15:4	16:1	16:12	17:17	17:18
18:1	18:7	18:8	18:13	18:25	21:7
21:9	21:11	22:7	25:5	25:22	25:38
26:8	27:5	28:17	29:2	29:5	

2 Samuel

2:21	3:13	3:14	5:2	7:5	7:13
7:23	8:4	9:11	11:12	12:3	12:4
13:13	14:11	15:2	15:16	16:18	18:1
18:3	18:4	18:12	18:15	19:9	19:14
19:17	19:43	20:3	20:21	21:6	21:16
21:18	23:8	24:3	24:12		

1 Kings

2:16	2:20	3:4	3:22	4:7	5:14
6:23	6:24	6:27	7:12	7:24	7:31
7:37	7:38	11:11	11:13	11:31	11:32
11:35	11:36	16:9	18:4	18:13	18:22
18:25	18:31	19:2	20:29	20:35	20:41
22:8	22:9	22:13			

2 Kings

4:39	4:43	5:5	5:18	7:8	8:26
11:4	11:9	11:15	11:19	13:7	14:7
15:13	15:19	17:28	19:22	20:9	20:10
23:33	24:14	25:1	25:25		

1Chronicles

6:61	11:11	11:12	12:14	12:38	13:1
16:15	17:11	17:12	17:21	18:4	19:6
21:3	21:5	21:10	21:17	22:10	22:14
23:11	24:6	28:6	29:1	29:7	29:21

2 Chronicles

1:6	3:16	4:3	4:7	4:8	5:13
6:9	6:42	14:1	15:6	18:7	18:12
22:2	25:5	25:11	25:12	26:2	27:5
28:6	30:24	32:12	32:30		

Ezra

3:1	6:17	7:22	10:16

Nehemiah

2:12	3:1	4:12	4:17	5:11	5:18
8:1	10:38	11:1	12:39		

Esther

1:7	3:9	4:11	9:10	9:12	9:13

Job

1:15	1:16	1:17	1:19	6:10	9:3
19:3	21:23	32:12	33:23	34:17	34:18
36:4					

Psalms

2:2	3:6	14:3	16:10	19:6	27:4
28:8	33:2	50:1	50:10	62:11	68:8
68:17	71:22	76:11	78:41	83:5	84:9

84:10	89:3	89:18	89:38	89:51	90:4
91:7	92:3	105:8	105:13	106:23	113:5
119:72	132:2	132:10	132:11	132:17	132:23
137:3	139:16	141:7	144:3	144:9	144:10
144:13	145:4				

Proverbs

9:10	11:24	13:7	17:10	21:12	30:3

Ecclesiastes

4:9	4:10	4:11	4:12	5:8	6:3
6:6	7:19	7:27	7:28	8:12	9:18

Song of Solomon

1:9	4:4	4:9	5:10	8:11	8:12

Isaiah

1:4	1:24	3:6	4:1	5:19	5:27
6:6	6:13	7:23	10:17	10:20	10:34
12:6	16:5	17:7	19:11	19:18	21:16
22:11	24:16	26:7	27:12	28:2	29:19
29:23	30:11	30:12	30:15	30:17	31:1
33:21	36:9	37:23	37:38	38:8	40:3
40:25	40:26	41:14	41:16	41:20	42:1
43:3	43:10	43:14	43:15	45:11	47:4
48:17	49:7	49:26	54:4	55:5	57:15
60:9	60:14	60:16	60:22	65:20	66:23

Jeremiah

3:14	5:1	9:3	24:2	32:18	33:26
39:1	41:1	41:2	4:8	41:19	42:7
46:12	50:29	51:5	52:4	52:12	

Ezekiel

24:1	29:1	33:21	34:17	34:22	34:23
37:17	37:19	37:22	37:24	39:7	40:5
40:6	40:7	40:12	40:13	40:19	40:23
40:27	40:47	41:13	41:14	41:15	42:2

42:4	42:8	45:15	46:7	47:3	47:4
47:5	48:1	48:2	48:3	48:4	48:5
48:6	48:7	48:23	48:24	48:25	48:26
48:27					

Daniel

1:12	1:14	1:15	1:20	2:9	4:23
5:1	7:9	7:10	7:13	7:14	7:20
7:24	8:3	8:9	8:22	9:25	9:26
11:5	11:7	11:12			

Hosea

1:11	5:3	6:9	11:9	11:12

Amos

4:7	6:9	6:12

Micah

6:7	6:9

Habakkuk

1:12

Haggai

2:15

Zechariah

3:9	8:19	8:23	11:7	11:8	14:9

Malachi

2:10	2:15

Matthew

2:2	3:3	3:11	5:19	5:29	5:30
5:36	5:41	10:23	10:29	10:40	12:6
12:41	13:37	18:12	18:13	18:24	18:28
18:29	19:5	19:6	19:17	20:12	21:24
23:8	23:10	23:23	24:2	24:40	24:41

25:1	25:18	25:24	25:32	26:40	26:64
27:38					

Mark

1:24	4:20	6:40	8:24	10:8	10:18
10:21	10:30	10:41	11:29	12:29	12:32
14:37	14:44	14:61	15:27		

Luke

1:35	1:49	3:14	3:16	4:34	6:29
7:19	7:27	8:8	9:48	10:42	11:31
11:32	11:40	11:46	12:1	12:52	13:8
14:31	15:4	15:7	15:8	15:10	16:7
16:13	17:12	17:17	17:31	17:34	18:12
19:13	19:16	19:17	19:24	19:25	19:44
21:6	21:8	23:18	23:33	23:35	

John

1:14	1:16	1:18	1:23	1:26	1:27
1:30	1:33	1:45	3:16	3:18	6:69
7:18	7:21	7:33	8:9	8:18	8:24
8:28	8:29	8:50	8:54	9:25	10:16
10:30	10:36	11:50	11:52	12:45	13:26
15:21	17:11	17:21	17:22	18:9	19:18
19:23	19:34	19:37			

Acts

2:1	2:27	3:14	4:26	4:32	7:52
12:10	13:25	13:35	13:37	17:26	19:29
21:20	22:16	22:19	24:21	26:11	26:12

Romans

3:10	3:30	4:15	4:19	5:12	5:14
5:15	5:16	5:17	5:18	5:19	8:20
9:10	11:3	11:30	12:4	12:5	13:9
14:2	14:6	14:19	15:6		

1 Corinthians

3:8	3:11	4:6	4:15	6:6	6:16
6:17	8:4	8:6	9:24	10:17	12:7
12:9	12:11	12:12	12:13	12:14	12:19
12:20	12:26	14:19	15:39	15:40	15:41

2 Corinthians

11:2	13:11

Galatians

3:2	3:16	3:20	3:28	4:24	6:5

Ephesians

1:6	1:10	2:3	2:14	2:15	2:16
2:18	3:6	4:4	4:5	4:6	4:7
4:25	5:31	5:33			

Philippians

1:27	2:2	3:13	4:15

Colossians

3:15

1 Timothy

2:5	3:2	3:12

Titus

1:12	3:3

Hebrews

7:2	7:4	7:5	7:6	7:7	7:8
7:9	7:26	9:24	10:12	10:14	11:12
11:16	11:17	12:22			

James

2:10	2:19	4:12

2 Peter

    3:8

1 John

2:11	2:20	4:9

The Revelation

1:3	1:18	2:10	5:11	6:21	11:13
11:17	12:3	13:2	13:3	14:14	15:7
16:5	17:1	17:3	17:7	17:12	17:13
17:16	18:8	18:10	18:17	18:19	20:2
20:3	20:4	20:5	20:6	20:7	21:9

Two and Equivalents

Genesis

1:16	4:19	6:19	6:20	7:2	7:20
9:22	11:10	13:11	15:10	19:1	19:8
19:12	19:15	19:30	21:27	21:31	22:3
22:6	22:8	22:22	25:23	27:9	27:36
29:16	31:33	31:37	31:38	31:41	32:7
32:10	32:14	32:22	33:1	34:25	37:9
40:2	40:5	41:1	41:32	41:50	44:27
45:6	46:27	48:1	48:5	49:14	

Exodus

2:13	4:9	18:3	18:6	20:45	25:18
26:7	26:8	26:17	26:18	27:7	28:11
29:1	29:38	31:18	32:15	34:1	34:4
34:29	36:13	38:18	38:26		

Leviticus

5:7	5:11	8:2	12:5	12:8	14:4
14:10	16:1	16:5	16:12	19:19	23:17
23:18	23:19				

Numbers

7:17	7:89	9:22	10:2	11:26	13:23
22:22	22:24	23:2	28:3	28:11	

Deuteronomy

3:8	3:21	4:13	4:47	5:22	9:10
9:11	9:15	9:17	10:1	10:3	14:6
17:6	19:15	19:17	21:15	25:13	25:14

Joshua

2:1	2:4	2:10	2:23	6:22	9:10
14:4	24:12				

Judges

7:25	8:12	9:44	11:37	15:13	16:3
16:28	16:29	17:2	19:3	19:6	19:8
19:10	20:45				

Ruth

1:1	1:5	1:7	1:8	1:19

1 Samuel

1:2	1:3	4:11	6:7	10:2	10:4
10:6	11:11	18:7	18:27	23:18	25:18
27:3	30:10	30:12	30:21		

2 Samuel

8:2	12:1	13:23	14:6	14:28	15:11
16:1	23:20				

1 Kings

2:5	2:32	3:16	3:25	5:11	5:12
6:25	6:32	8:19	9:10	9:11	10:16
12:28	16:21	18:4	18:23	20:27	21:10

2 Kings

1:14	2:6	2:8	2:11	4:42	5:22

7:14	10:4	10:8	11:7	17:16	18:23
23:12	25:4				

1 Chronicles

11:22	18:4	23:24	27:23

2 Chronicles

2:10	3:8	3:11	3:15	5:10	8:1
28:8	28:11	31:17			

Nehemiah

11:16	12:31	12:40

Esther

2:21	2:23	6:2	9:27

Job

11:6	13:20

Psalms

62:11

Proverbs

24:22	30:7

Ecclesiastes

4:6	4:9	4:11	4:12

Song of Solomon

4:5	7:3	8:12

Isaiah

7:4	7:16	7:21	22:11	36:8

Jeremiah

2:13	3:14	24:1	28:3	28:11	22:24
34:18	39:4	52:7	52:20		

Ezekiel

1:11	1:23	4:10	21:19	21:21	23:2
35:10	37:22	40:41	41:10	41:18	41:24
45:15	47:13				

Daniel

7:4	8:3	8:7	8:20	11:27	12:5

Hosea

6:2

Amos

1:1	3:3	3:12	6:2

Jonah

4:11

Zechariah

4:3	4:11	4:12	4:14	5:9	6:1
6:13	11:7	14:4			

Matthew

2:16	4:18	4:21	4:41	6:24	8:28
9:27	10:29	14:17	17:24	18:8	18:9
18:15	18:16	18:19	18:20	19:5	19:6
20:21	20:24	20:30	21:1	21:28	21:31
22:40	24:40	24:41	25:15	25:17	26:2
26:37	26:61	27:21	27:38	27:51	28:16

Mark

5:13	6:7	6:14	6:38	9:43	9:45
9:47	10:8	11:1	12:42	14:1	14:13
15:27	15:38	16:2			

Luke

2:24	3:11	5:2	7:18	7:41	9:14
9:30	9:32	10:1	10:35	12:6	12:52
14:31	15:11	16:13	17:34	17:35	18:10

| 19:29 | 21:2 | 22:38 | 23:32 | 23:45 | 24:4 |
| 24:9 | 24:13 | 24:33 | 24:35 | | |

John

| 1:35 | 1:37 | 4:40 | 4:43 | 6:9 | 8:17 |
| 11:6 | 11:18 | 19:18 | 19:40 | 20:12 | |

Acts

1:10	1:23	1:26	2:14	7:26	9:38
10:7	12:6	13:4	15:22	19:10	19:22
19:34	21:33	23:23	24:27	28:30	

1 Corinthians

| 6:16 | 14:27 |

Galatians

| 4:22 | 4:24 |

Ephesians

| 2:15 | 5:31 |

Philippians

1:23

Hebrews

| 6:18 | 11:37 |

The Revelation

| 9:16 | 11:3 | 11:4 | 11:10 | 12:14 | 13:11 |
| 19:20 | | | | | |

Three and Equivalents

Genesis

| 6:10 | 7:13 | 9:19 | 14:4 | 15:9 | 17:20 |
| 18:2 | 25:16 | 29:2 | 29:34 | 30:36 | 34:25 |

35:22	38:24	40:10	40:13	40:16	40:18
40:19	41:46	42:13	42:17	45:22	

Exodus

2:2	3:18	5:3	8:27	10:22	10:23
15:22	15:27	21:11	21:32	23:14	23:17
24:4	27:1	27:14	28:1	28:21	32:28
34:23	34:24	39:14			

Leviticus

19:23	24:5	25:21

Numbers

1:44	4:3	7:3	7:84	7:86	7:87
10:33	11:31	17:2	17:6	20:29	22:28
22:32	22:33	24:10	29:17	31:5	33:9
35:14					

Deuteronomy

1:23	4:41	14:28	16:16	17:6	19:2
19:3	34:8				

Joshua

1:11	2:16	2:22	3:2	3:12	4:3
4:4	4:8	4:9	4:20	8:3	8:25
9:16	15:14	18:4	18:24	19:15	

Judges

7:16	7:20	9:43	10:4	12:9	14:11
14:12	14:14	14:19	19:4	19:29	20:31
20:39	21:10				

1 Samuel

1:24	2:13	4:10	9:20	9:22	10:3
11:8	11:11	13:1	13:17	17:13	20:20
20:41	30:12	30:13	31:6	31:8	

2 Samuel

2:15	2:18	5:4	6:1	6:11	10:6
13:38	17:1	18:14	20:4	21:1	23:8
23:9	23:13	23:16	23:18	23:23	24:12
24:13					

1 Kings

2:39	4:7	4:22	4:26	5:13	6:36
7:25	7:26	9:25	10:20	10:22	10:26
11:30	12:5	12:12	17:21	18:31	19:19
22:1					

2 Kings

2:17	3:10	11:5	13:18	13:19	13:25
17:5	18:10	23:31	24:1	24:8	25:18

1 Chronicles

10:6	11:12	11:15	11:18	11:20	11:25
11:42	12:4	12:18	12:39	13:14	21:10
21:12	23:3				

2 Chronicles

1:14	4:4	8:13	9:19	9:21	9:25
10:12	11:17	12:3	20:25	31:16	35:7

Ezra

6:4	6:17	8:15	8:24	8:25	8:32
8:35	10:8	10:9			

Nehemiah

2:11

Esther

2:12	4:11	4:16

Job

1:4	1:17	2:11	32:1	32:3	32:5
33:29	42:3				

Psalms
    60:1

Proverbs

22:20	30:15	30:18	30:21	30:29

Ecclesiastes

4:12	16:14	17:16	20:3

Jeremiah

36:23	38:10	52:24

Ezekiel

14:14	14:16	14:18	21:14	40:10	40:17
40:21	41:6	42:3	47:13	48:31	48:32
48:33	48:34				

Daniel

1:5	3:23	3:24	4:29	6:2	6:7
6:10	6:12	6:13	7:5	7:8	7:20
7:24	10:2	10:3	11:2		

Amos

1:3	1:6	1:9	1:11	1:13	2:1
2:4	2:6	4:4	4:7		

Jonah

1:17	3:3

Zechariah

11:8	11:12	11:13

Matthew

9:20	10:1	10:2	10:5	11:11	12:40
13:8	13:23	14:20	15:32	17:4	18:20
19:28	20:17	26:14	26:15	26:20	26:34

26:47	26:53	26:61	26:75	27:3	27:9
27:40	27:63				

Mark

3:13	3:14	3:16	4:8	4:10	4:20
5:25	6:43	8:2	8:19	8:32	9:5
9:31	9:35	10:32	10:34	11:1	14:10
14:17	14:20	14:30	14:43	14:58	14:72
15:29					

Luke

1:56	2:46	3:23	4:25	6:13	8:1
8:42	8:43	9:1	9:12	9:17	9:33
10:36	11:5	12:52	13:7	18:31	22:3
22:30	22:34	22:47	22:61		

John

2:19	2:20	6:13	6:19	6:67	6:70
6:71	11:9	13:38	20:24		

Acts

3:1	5:7	6:2	7:8	7:21	9:9
10:3	10:16	10:19	10:30	11:10	11:11
17:2	19:7	19:8	20:3	20:31	24:11
25:1	26:7	28:7	28:11	28:12	28:15
28:17					

1 Corinthians

13:13	14:27	15:5

2 Corinthians

11:25	12:8

Galatians

1:18

Hebrews

11:23

James
    1:1

1 John
    5:7   5:8

The Revelation

6:6	8:13	9:18	12:1	16:13	16:19
21:12	21:13	21:14	21:21	22:2	

Four and Equivalents

Genesis

2:10	2:14	7:4	7:12	7:17	8:6
14:4	14:11	15:13	15:16	23:15	23:16
25:20	26:40	32:6	33:1	50:3	

Exodus

16:35	20:5	24:18	25:12	26:32	27:2
28:17	34:28	36:36			

Leviticus

11:20	11:21	11:27	11:42	19:24

Numbers

13:25	14:33	14:34	32:13

Deuteronomy

2:7	8:2	8:4	9:9	9:11	9:18
9:25	10:10	25:3	29:5		

Joshua

4:13	5:6	14:7

Judges

4:13	5:8	5:31	8:28	9:34	11:40
12:14	13:1	14:15	19:2	20:2	20:17
20:47	21:12				

1 Samuel

4:2	17:16	22:2	25:13	27:7	30:10
30:17					

2 Samuel

2:10	5:4	10:18	12:6	15:7

1 Kings

4:26	6:37	7:2	7:30	7:34	7:42
11:42	18:19	19:8	22:6		

2 Kings

7:3	8:9	10:30	25:3

1 Chronicles

4:13	9:24	9:25	9:30	13:3	18:5
18:15	19:18	23:5	26:11	26:17	26:18
29:27					

Ezra

6:17

Nehemiah

5:15	6:4	9:21

Job

1:19	42:16

Psalms

95:10

Proverbs

29:11	29:12	29:13	30:15	30:18	30:21
30:24	30:29				

Isaiah

11:12	17:6

Jeremiah

15:3	36:28	49:36	52:21

Ezekiel

1:5	1:6	1:8	1:10	1:15	1:16
1:17	1:18	7:2	10:9	10:10	10:11
10:12	10:14	10:21	14:21	29:11	29:12
29:13	37:9	40:41	40:42	42:20	43:20
46:21					

Daniel

1:17	2:40	3:25	7:2	7:3	7:6
7:7	7:17	7:23	8:8	8:22	11:2
11:4					

Amos

1:3	1:6	2:1	2:4

Jonah

3:4

Zechariah

1:18	1:20	2:6	6:1	6:3	6:5

Matthew

4:2	14:25	15:38	16:10	17:27	24:31

Mark

2:3	6:48	8:9	8:20	11:3	13:27

Luke

| 4:2 | 16:6 | 19:8 | | | |

John

| 4:35 | 11:17 | 11:39 | 19:23 | | |

Acts

1:3	4:22	5:36	7:6	7:23	7:36
7:42	10:11	10:12	10:30	11:5	12:4
13:18	13:21	21:9	21:23	23:13	23:21
27:29					

2 Corinthians

11:24

Hebrews

| 3:9 | 3:17 | | | | |

The Revelation

4:7	4:8	5:6	5:8	5:14	6:1
6:6	6:7	6:8	7:1	7:2	7:11
8:12	9:14	9:15	14:3	15:7	16:8
20:8					

Five and Equivalents

Genesis

| 14:9 | 31:41 | 43:34 | 45:6 | 45:11 | 45:22 |
| 46:22 | 47:2 | | | | |

Exodus

| 22:1 | 26:3 | 26:5 | 27:10 | 38:12 | 38:13 |

Leviticus

| 23:16 | 26:8 | 27:3 | 27:5 | 27:6 | |

Numbers

3:47	4:13	7:17	8:25	18:16	29:3
31:8	31:28	31:30	31:47		

Deuteronomy

22:29

Joshua

7:21	8:12	10:5	10:16	10:17	10:22
10:26	13:3				

Judges

3:3	18:12	18:7	18:14	18:17	20:45

1 Samuel

6:14	6:16	6:18	17:5	17:40	21:3
25:42					

2 Samuel

4:4	15:1	21:8	24:9	24:24	

1 Kings

1:5	6:31	7:16	7:39	7:49	8:65
10:26	18:4	20:1	22:31		

2 Kings

1:9	1:10	1:11	1:12	1:13	2:7
2:16	2:17	7:13	13:7	13:19	15:20
15:25	25:19				

1 Chronicles

2:4	3:20	4:42	5:21	7:3	19:7
29:7					

2 Chronicles

1:14	3:9	3:11	4:6	12:2	13:17
13:21	35:9				

Job
    42:12

Isaiah
    3:3   17:6   19:18   30:7

Ezekiel
    40:15   41:2   42:16   42:17   42:18   42:19
    42:20

Haggai
    2:16

Matthew
    14:17   14:19   14:21   16:9   25:2   25:15
    25:16

Mark
    6:38   6:41   6:44   8:19

Luke
    1:24   7:41   9:14   9:15   9:16   12:6
    12:52   14:19   16:28   19:18   19:19

John
    4:18   5:2   6:9   6:10   8:57

Acts
    4:4   19:9   20:6   24:1   27:33

1 Corinthians
    10:8   14:19   15:6

2 Corinthians
    11:24   12:2

Galatians
    2:1

The Revelation

9:5	9:10	17:10

Six and Equivalents

Genesis

7:6	7:11	13:1	25:26	30:20	31:41

Exodus

13:27	14:7	16:5	16:26	16:29	20:9
20:11	21:2	23:10	23:12	24:16	25:32
26:22	27:14	28:10	31:15	31:17	34:21
35:2	37:18				

Leviticus

23:3	25:3	25:21	27:3	27:7

Numbers

7:3	7:42	7:88	11:21	29:29	35:4
35:6	35:13				

Deuteronomy

3:4	5:13	15:12	15:18	16:8

Joshua

6:3	6:14	13:30

Judges

3:31	8:10	12:6	12:7	18:11	18:16
18:7	20:47				

Ruth

3:15	3:17

1 Samuel

13:1	13:5	13:15	14:2	17:7	23:13
27:2	30:9				

2 Samuel

2:31	6:13	15:18	21:20

1 Kings

4:13	4:22	6:2	10:19	10:20	10:29
11:16	16:23				

2 Kings

2:24	5:5	10:14	11:3	13:9	14:13
18:10	20:6	25:19			

1 Chronicles

2:23	20:6	21:25	23:4	26:17	27:9

2 Chronicles

1:17	2:2	3:3	9:15	9:18	9:19
11:21	12:3	22:12	25:23	29:33	

Ezra

6:15

Esther

2:12

Job

5:19	42:2

Proverbs

6:16

Song of Solomon

3:7	6:8

Isaiah
6:2   38:5

Jeremiah
34:14   52:25

Ezekiel
4:11   8:1   9:2   40:5   40:12   40:14
41:1   41:3   41:8   46:1   46:4

Haggai
1:1

Matthew
13:8   17:1   20:6   27:45

Mark
4:8   9:2   15:33

Luke
1:26   1:36   3:1   13:14   23:44

John
2:6   4:6   12:1   19:14

Acts
11:12   27:37

Galatians
1:18

1 Timothy
5:9

The Revelation
4:8   4:10   5:8   6:12   9:13   9:14
11:16   13:5   13:18   16:2   19:4

Seven and Equivalents

Genesis

2:2	2:3	4:15	4:24	7:2	7:3
7:4	7:10	8:10	21:29	21:29	29:18
29:20	29:27	29:30	31:23	33:3	41:2
41:4	41:5	41:6	41:7	41:18	41:19
41:20	41:22	41:23	41:24	41:26	41:27
41:29	41:34	41:36	41:47	41:48	41:53
41:54	46:25	46:27	50:3	50:10	

Exodus

1:5	2:16	7:25	12:15	12:16	12:19
13:6	13:7	15:27	16:26	16:27	16:29
16:30	20:10	20:11	21:2	22:30	23:11
23:12	23:15	24:1	24:9	24:16	25:37
29:30	29:35	29:37	31:15	31:17	34:18
34:21	35:2	37:23			

Leviticus

4:6	4:7	4:17	8:11	8:33	8:35
12:2	13:4	13:5	13:6	13:21	13:26
13:27	13:31	13:32	13:33	13:34	13:50
13:51	13:54	14:7	14:8	14:9	14:16
14:27	14:38	14:39	14:51	15:13	15:19
15:24	15:28	16:14	16:19	16:29	22:27
23:3	23:6	23:8	23:15	23:16	23:18
23:24	23:27	23:34	23:36	23:39	23:40
23:41	23:42	25:4	25:8	25:9	25:20
26:18	26:21	26:24	26:28		

Numbers

6:9	7:13	7:19	7:25	7:31	7:37
7:43	7:48	7:49	8:2	11:16	11:24
11:25	12:14	12:15	13:22	19:11	19:12
19:14	19:16	19:19	23:1	23:4	23:14

23:29	28:11	28:17	28:19	28:21	28:24
28:25	28:27	29:1	29:2	29:7	29:8
29:12	29:32	29:36	31:19	31:24	33:9

Deuteronomy

5:14	7:1	10:22	15:1	15:9	15:12
16:3	16:4	16:8	16:9	16:13	16:15
28:7	28:25	31:10			

Joshua

| 6:4 | 6:6 | 6:13 | 6:15 | 6:16 | 18:5 |

Judges

1:7	6:1	6:25	8:30	9:2	9:4
9:5	9:18	9:24	9:56	12:9	12:14
14:12	14:17	14:18	16:7	16:8	16:13
16:19	20:15	20:16			

Ruth

| 4:15 |

1 Samuel

| 2:5 | 6:1 | 6:19 | 10:8 | 11:3 | 13:8 |
| 16:10 | 31:13 | | | | |

2 Samuel

| 8:4 | 10:18 | 12:18 | 21:6 | 21:9 | 24:15 |

1 Kings

| 5:15 | 6:6 | 6:38 | 7:17 | 8:65 | 11:3 |
| 18:43 | 18:44 | 19:18 | 20:29 | | |

2 Kings

3:9	3:26	4:35	5:10	5:14	8:1
8:2	8:3	10:1	10:6	10:7	11:4
24:16					

1 Chronicles

2:15	9:25	10:12	15:26	18:4	19:18
21:24	29:4				

2 Chronicles

2:2	5:3	7:8	7:9	13:9	15:11
29:21	30:21	30:22	30:33	30:24	31:7
35:17					

Ezra

3:1	3:6	3:22	7:7	7:8	7:14

Nehemiah

7:73	8:2	8:14	8:18	10:31

Esther

1:5	1:10	1:14	2:9	2:16

Job

1:2	1:3	2:13	5:19	42:8	42:13

Psalms

12:6	90:10	119:164

Proverbs

6:16	6:31	9:1	24:16	26:16	26:25

Isaiah

23:15	23:17	30:26

Jeremiah

15:9	25:11	25:12	28:17	29:10	34:14
41:1	52:25				

Ezekiel

3:15	3:16	8:11	20:1	30:20	39:9
39:12	39:14	40:22	43:25	44:26	45:20
45:21	45:23	45:25			

Daniel

3:19	4:16	4:23	4:25	4:32	9:2
9:24	9:25	9:26	9:27		

Micah

5:5

Zechariah

1:12	3:9	4:2	4:10	7:5	8:19

Matthew

12:45	15:34	15:36	15:37	16:10	18:21
18:22	22:25	22:26	22:28		

Mark

8:5	8:6	8:8	8:20	12:20	12:22
12:23	16:9				

Luke

2:36	8:2	11:26	17:4	20:29	20:31
20:33					

John

4:52

Acts

6:3	13:19	20:6	21:4	21:8	21:27
23:23					

Romans

11:4

Hebrews

4:4	11:30

2 Peter

2:5

Jude
> 1:14

The Revelation

1:4	1:5	1:11	1:12	1:16	1:20
2:1	3:1	4:5	5:1	5:5	5:6
6:1	8:1	8:2	8:6	10:3	10:4
10:7	11:13	11:15	12:3	13:2	15:1
15:6	15:7	15:8	16:1	16:7	17:1
17:3	17:7	17:9	17:10	17:11	21:9

Eight and Equivalents

Genesis

7:11	8:4	17:2	21:4	22:23	37:2
47:28					

Exodus

7:7	22:30	26:25	36:30

Leviticus

9:1	12:3	14:10	15:14	15:29	22:27
23:36	23:39	25:22			

Numbers

6:10	7:8	7:54	29:29	29:35

Judges

3:8	3:30	8:26	20:15

1 Samuel
> 17:12

2 Samuel

19:32	19:35	23:8	24:9

1 Kings
5:15	6:1	7:10	12:21	12:32	12:33

2 Kings
6:25	8:17	10:24	22:1	24:12

1 Chronicles
26:30	27:11

2 Chronicles
2:2	7:9	13:3	14:8	21:5	21:20
26:17	29:17	34:1	34:3		

Nehemiah
8:18

Psalms
90:10

Ecclesiastes
11:2

Song of Solomon
6:8

Jeremiah
32:9	41:5	41:15

Ezekiel
40:9	40:31	40:41	43:27

Daniel
5:31	9:25	9:26

Micah
5:5

Zechariah
    1:1

Mark
    6:37

Luke
    1:59   2:21   9:28   16:6   16:7

John
    6:7

Acts
    7:8   9:33   25:6

Philippians
    3:5

1 Peter
    3:20

The Revelation
    17:11

Nine and Equivalents

Genesis
    17:1   17:24

Leviticus
    23:32   25:22

Numbers
    29:26

Judges
 3:14   4:3   10:8   20:25

1 Samuel
 17:4

2 Samuel
 8:13   20:30   24:8

2 Kings
 17:6   18:10   23:23   25:1   25:3   25:17

1 Chronicles
 3:8   26:32

2 Chronicles
 11:1   35:19

Ezra
 10:9

Nehemiah
 11:1

Jeremiah
 32:11   36:9   39:1   39:2   52:4   52:6

Ezekiel
 24:1

Daniel
 3:1

Haggai
 2:10   2:18

Zechariah
 7:1

Matthew

    18:12   18:13

Luke

    10:1   10:17   13:4   13:11   13:16   15:4
    15:7   17:7

Acts

    2:15   23:23

Appendix F

Bibliography

The Books Called Apocrypha: According to the Authorized Version. New York: Oxford University, 1963.

The Living Bible. Illinois: Tyndale House, 1971.

Lucas, Jerry and Del Washburn. *Theomatics: God's Best Kept Secret Revealed.* New York: Stein and Day, 1977.

The New Interpreter's Bible in Twelve Volumes. Nashville: Abington Press, 1995.

The New Scofield Reference Edition: Holy Bible. New York: Oxford University, 1967.

Ryrie, Charles Caldwell. *The Ryrie Study Bible.* Chicago: Moody, 1994.

978-0-595-41150-4
0-595-41150-9

Made in the USA
Middletown, DE
31 October 2019